Memphis
C H R O N I C L E S

Memphis CHRONICLES

Bits of History from the *Best Times*

JOHN E. HARKINS

THE
History
PRESS

Published by The History Press
Charleston, SC 29403
www.historypress.net

First published 2009

ISBN 978-1-5402-2012-7

Library of Congress Cataloging-in-Publication Data

Harkins, John E., 1938-
Memphis chronicles : bits of history from the best times / John E. Harkins.
p. cm.
Includes bibliographical references and index.
ISBN 978-1-59629-714-2 (alk. paper)
1. Memphis (Tenn.)--History. I. Title.
F444.M557H36 2009
976.8'19--dc22
2009026248

The author lovingly dedicates this little book to his wife, Georgia S. Harkins, and to his brothers, Charlie, Tommy and Jerry Harkins.

CONTENTS

CONTENTS

Preface

WHERE IS CLIO HIDING?

Memphis and Shelby County history sources and history-promoting institutions are generally difficult for local history neophytes to locate. Even so, it has very often been geographical transplants who have become the most devoted students of our local history and have most effectively researched and chronicled our city's past. Beginning in the nineteenth century with James D. Davis and John M. Keating, and continuing through the twentieth century with Paul R. Coppock, Enoch Mitchell, Robert Sigafoos and Perre Magness, many of our most beloved bards have been non-natives. Natives and newcomers alike deserve an easier and most interesting path to our locale's past.

The contents of this little book are drawn nearly exclusively from columns written for a series called "The Best in Memphis History." These articles have appeared monthly in the *Best Times* magazine over the last five years. *Best Times* publisher Lester Gingold says of the series, "The John Harkins monthly column in the *Best Times* has consistently been a favorite with our sixty thousand readers. Harkins brings history alive with his writings, and we have nominated him for 'Mature Media Awards' recognition."

The major point in writing such a local history column has been to lead readers to the best that is available in Memphis-area history. Even so, many of the essays' topics have sprung from my personal encounters with interesting and incidental milestones and events. In that sense, many of these essays are folksy, rough vehicles and guides for helping to popularize and promote our area's past. Many of the essays are meant simply to lead readers to worthwhile local authors, books, articles, institutions, museums, events, monuments, parks and other historical sites.

These *Best Times* columns also seek to personalize history in a way that confirms that we are all historians to one extent or another. This is demonstrated by the fact that some essays and images depict personal experiences, interacting with aspects of history close by. Helping readers to make the connection between their personal, prosaic-seeming pasts and the larger, more formal historical pageant helps them take an important conceptual leap. History is alive and surrounds all of us at all times.

A possible problem with the republication of these essays is that they were written to appear in a periodical. Often they comment on some aspect of the "state of history" in the Memphis area at a particular point in time. I have reviewed all of the essays and attempted to retain only information of enduring value as far as is practicable. Of necessity, there is significant overlap and some duplication of information among these writings.

To contact institutions or individuals referred to in this book's essays, interested parties should call the Memphis Public Library's Linc Department at (901) 415-2700 or conduct keyword searches online. Another superb source of such information would be through the West Tennessee Historical Society's website at www.wths.tn.org, its officials and its various online hyperlinks.

ACKNOWLEDGEMENTS

I would like to thank Walter D. Wills III for arranging and participating in the meeting from which "The Best in Memphis History" feature emerged and for providing grant support for its publication. Likewise, Publisher Lester Gingold and Editor Tom Jordan have provided generous moral support for the column and for the publication of *Historic Shelby County* in July 2008. Edwin G. Frank, Chris Ratliff and Sharon Banker, all of the University of Memphis Special Collections Department, have very generously provided facts and images electronically and on short notice so that no *Best Times* deadlines have been missed (or even bruised). Thanks also to the Memphis University School and the Historical Publishing Network for granting permission to reprint materials that I wrote for *MUS Today* and *Historic Shelby County*, respectively. Most special thanks to the Memphis University School for permitting me to work on this book project during my year as the school's writer in residence.

PART I

Sources for Memphis-Area History

Memphis-Area History and the West Tennessee Historical Society

The West Tennessee Historical Society (WTHS) is one of the Mid-South's least conspicuous yet most beneficial educational and recreational amenities. It is the umbrella heritage organization for the Western "Grand Division" of Tennessee and is a true cultural gem. Through its antecedent organizations, WTHS dates back to 1857, when "the Old Folks of Shelby County" began meeting regularly for fellowship and programs. At these gatherings, residents who had arrived in Shelby County during the 1820s and '30s told the stories of their pioneer days.

In the Civil War's aftermath, three successive local history groups had a Confederate historical emphasis. In the 1910s, the last of these groups morphed into the Memphis Historical Society (MHS). In 1935, the MHS broadened its geographical scope to include all twenty-one counties of West Tennessee. Reflecting West Tennessee's population distribution, however, somewhat more than half of the society's historical emphasis has stayed focused on Memphis and Shelby County. Consequently, there is no separate historical society for either Memphis or Shelby County. Most of the other West Tennessee counties, however, do have their own county and/or town historical or genealogical societies.

From its inception, WTHS has sponsored and scheduled periodic history programs. Such programming includes both formal papers and audiovisual presentations devoted to almost any aspects of West Tennessee's history. Since 1996, Memphis University School (6191 Park Avenue) has hosted the society's regular monthly meetings. The November and March meetings are held in the Martin and Jackson, Tennessee areas, respectively. Occasionally, regular meetings are held at nearby historical sites.

The West Tennessee Historical
Society.

At least as important as the society's programs has been the publication of its annual journal. Since 1947, WTHS has published an anthology of formal papers, notes, documents and book reviews relating to West Tennessee. Nearly the entire run of the society's sixty-two volumes of the *WTHS Papers* is available digitally via the Shelby County Register's website.

Almost as important as publishing its *Papers* is the society's work in promoting, sponsoring and publishing books and reprints related to the area's history. Such books include: *The Old Folks Record*; J. Harvey Mathes's *The Old Guard in Grey*; Judge J.P. Young's *Standard History of Memphis, Tennessee*; James D. Davis's *The History of the City of Memphis* (facsimile reprint edited by James E. Roper); and John E. Harkins's *Metropolis of the American Nile* and *Historic Shelby County*. WTHS has also bought up inventories of excellent remaindered books, keeping them available for purchase at bargain prices. Examples include Robert A. Sigafoos's *Cotton Row to Beale Street* and Paul R. Coppock's six-volume set of Memphis-area historical vignettes.

The society's other major functions include sanctioning and erecting historical markers, helping preserve historical structures and sites and collecting and preserving publications and documents bearing on West Tennessee history. The WTHS manuscript collections and rare books are permanently housed in the Special Collections Department at the University of Memphis.

Finally, WTHS serves as a referral network and a clearinghouse for building cooperation and sharing information about events bearing on West Tennessee's past. In short, WTHS is the strongest single resource for all aspects of Memphis-area history.

MEMPHIS SKETCHES COPPOCK

Paul Coppock's six hardcover books on Memphis-area history were compiled from his decades of news columns. They provide the broadest and most detailed narratives of the Mid-South's past. *Courtesy of West Tennessee Historical Society.*

To learn more about your West Tennessee Historical Society, please visit the society's website at www.wths.tn.org or contact the society directly via PO Box 111046, Memphis, TN, 38119. New members are always welcome.

Our City's Legacy of Splendid Journalists/Historians

Paul R. Coppock's Contributions and the End of a Vital Tradition

The late, great *Washington Post* publisher Phil Graham purportedly coined the phrase "News is the first draft of history." Although Graham's proposition may be debated, there is no denying that Memphis has been blessed with a string of journalists/historians who have brilliantly chronicled our community's past. The most notable of these would include John M. Keating, Joe Curtis, Thomas Fauntleroy, Paul R. Coppock and Perre Magness. Incidentally, each of these worthies also contributed broadly to other spheres of civic betterment.

Colonel J.M. Keating is the true father of Memphis history. As editor and part owner of the *Memphis Appeal*, he wrote a stirring, firsthand account of the *History of the* [1878] *Yellow Fever Epidemic* in Memphis. About a decade later, he penned the first volume of a wonderfully detailed *History of the City of Memphis and Shelby County* (O.F. Vedder completed the second volume). Although Keating included many persistent nineteenth-century myths, the wealth of detail and elegant prose in his *Memphis* history earned it a facsimile reprint in the 1970s.

In 1897, a year after Keating left Memphis, fledgling steamboat pilot Joe Curtis began writing for the *Commercial Appeal* (*CA*) and began his assent to prominence as our area's history guru. "Captain Joe" portrayed the romance of life and history on the Mississippi River for more than fifty years. His "In the Pilothouse" column was a favorite during much of that time. He also initiated the *CA*'s still popular "News of Bygone Days" feature. An extremely gifted and prolific storyteller, Curtis wrote folklore and fiction, as well as history. He sustained an enthusiastic readership until his health failed in 1958.

Captain (army rank in World War I) Thomas Fauntleroy, writer and editor at the *CA* from 1921 to 1939, had a phenomenal memory and a great grasp of this area's past. His most significant contribution to Memphis history, however, would be his unpublished, indexed chronology of the *Commercial Appeal* and its antecedent newspapers between about 1840 and 1924. Memphis's research libraries have copies of "the Fauntleroy Index," a vital tool for local history researchers.

Paul Coppock's Legacy for Local History

Paul R. Coppock's columns and his six hardcover books have probably had a greater and more positive impact on local history consciousness than the work of any other individual. I have always lauded Coppock's works, and on a personal level, I held him in warm regard and high esteem. His local history legacy just keeps on giving.

I had read some of Coppock's works before ever meeting him. I eagerly read his newspaper columns and *Memphis Sketches*, the first anthology of his articles. We even gave copies of *Sketches* to most of our relatives for Christmas in 1978. The following year, I was working at the City/County Archives and in the History Department of the public library. In those capacities, I sometimes pulled research materials for Mr. Coppock and we struck up a casual acquaintance. Shortly thereafter, I was gulled into serving as the West Tennessee Historical Society's "general arrangements chairman" for a book-signing party to launch Paul's second book, *Memphis Memoirs*. We staged a fun, successful event, and Paul appreciated my role in organizing the affair.

In addition to signing books that day, Paul was interviewed by one of our local television personalities. When the silky-voiced young man made a passing reference to "Boss Crump," Coppock immediately took him to task. Paul barked that people who truly knew Memphis history never referred to Crump in that fashion. He was "Mr. Crump" or "E.H. Crump," or even "Main and Adams." Paul's certitude and earnestness showed his passion for our history and for historical accuracy.

As Paul's health declined in the early 1980s, he had to give up writing his column. He died not long afterward. His widow, Helen, was determined to keep his legacy alive. She edited and published all of his remaining news columns in a four-volume series entitled *Paul R. Coppock's Mid South* (co-edited by Charles W. Crawford).

Prominent local historians still wax eloquent in praising Paul Coppock's books. Perre Magness, whose *Commercial Appeal* column "Past Times" appeared weekly for sixteen years, calls them "indispensable for understanding Memphis-area history." County historian Ed Williams describes them as "highly readable standard works that every Mid-South history fan should own." Jeanne Crawford, former director for the Fontaine House and Davies Manor, says that they are lively books that "continue to resonate with readers." Ed Frank, special collections curator at the University of Memphis, predicts that "anyone interested in our area's history will enjoy Coppock's books." Taken together, Paul's books are indeed the best and broadest source for popularly written Mid-South history.

Remarkably, all six of Coppock's books are available in several local bookstores. All six volumes are also available—in boxed sets only and at a very steep discount—through the West Tennessee Historical Society. For more information, go online to www.wths.tn.org or contact Mr. Bill Detling at DETLING2@aol.com or by phone at (901) 683-3854.

Old Shelby County Magazine

A Final Offer

I noted in this column almost two years ago that *Old Shelby County Magazine* (*OSC*) had ceased publication. Its editors, Cathy Marcinko and Lydia Spencer, had published their informative and entertaining magazine for five years, creating fifty-eight issues of a splendid amenity for Memphis-area history buffs. The magazine's art was delicious, very imitative of nineteenth-century illustrations and advertisements. The humor and recipes were intermixed and contained much good fun. The stories ranged from the quite scandalous to the sublime.

The editors themselves wrote many of *OSC*'s cover stories, but local historians, with considerable expertise on the topics that they covered, also wrote a great deal of the content. The editors even let me include a very brief sketch of the Memphis University School in the issue that focused on Hutchison School's century of service. Many of the other stories were popularly penned distillations of information that had appeared in the *West Tennessee Historical Society Papers* and other more formal history journals. Feature articles included stories about Marcus Winchester, Davy Crockett, Raleigh Springs, Richard Halliburton, the *Sultana*, Frances Wright, the Bolton-Dickens Feud, Nathan Bedford Forrest, Elizabeth Avery Meriwether,

ONLY 50¢

No. 48

OLD SHELBY COUNTY
MAGAZINE
HISTORY, HUMOR AND FOLK WAYS OF THE MID-SOUTH

Mrs. Meriwether Returns!

Memphis's indomitable heroine of the Civil War is back with the story of the "Sugar Lady" and a refugee's Christmas in 1863

Elizabeth Avery Meriwether is a favorite Memphis heroine. *Old Shelby County*'s editors justifiably celebrated her versatility and effectiveness in articles drawn from her memoir, *Recollections of Ninety-Two Years. Courtesy of* Old Shelby County *magazine.*

Also in this issue: President Lincoln Pardons a Turkey

ONLY 50¢

NO. 43

OLD SHELBY COUNTY MAGAZINE

HISTORY, HUMOR AND FOLK WAYS OF WEST TENNESSEE

Forrest

Among the sons of the South, there are few names more loved or hated than that of Nathan Bedford Forrest. He was a man who fought fiercely to win, but lost most of his own life's battles. His final battle, for redemption, is one that, for many, is still an open question.

Confederate general Nathan Bedford Forrest is undoubtedly the most controversial figure in Mid-South history. Venerated by local whites a century ago, he is currently disparaged by the politically correct. *Courtesy of* Old Shelby County *magazine.*

Also in this Issue—*The Story of Blind Tom* & *A Hope Brewster Update!*

the Daughters of the Emerald Island, Confederate spy Ginny Moon and ever so many more. *OSC* usually included two solid local history stories in every month's issue.

As Marcinko and Spencer prepared to give up publishing *OSC*, they made every reasonable effort to find some other entity to continue its publication. Alas, they found no takers. They gave their subscribers and members of various local history organizations the opportunity to buy the discounted remaining issues of their inventory. To our siblings' delight, my wife and I gave each of them a complete run of the magazine. When sales slowed to a stop, the owners gave their remaining inventory to Memphis Heritage, Inc. However, Marcinko and Spencer still own the reproduction rights to their magazine. Perhaps *OSC*'s most interesting stories will be grouped together thematically and republished at some point in the not-too-distant future. The magazine's stories are far too good to be lost to Memphis-area history buffs.

Professor Mitchell

State and Local Historian Extraordinaire

Many Memphians of long standing, if they also have long memories, are apt to recall the personality, career and community impact of Memphis State professor Enoch L. Mitchell. Born in Guntown, Mississippi, Mitchell grew up in Fayette County, Tennessee, was educated at West Tennessee State Teachers' College (WTSTC), taught history at Memphis State College (MSC) and later chaired the History Department of Memphis State University (MSU). Older Memphians will also recognize that WTSTC, MSC and MSU are each direct, lineal ancestors of today's University of Memphis.

After earning his bachelor's degree in 1929, Mitchell served as superintendent of the Fayette County Schools and did graduate work at Peabody College in Nashville. By 1939, he had earned his master's degree, and he returned to his alma mater to teach history. In 1952, with postwar growth and the college's expansion underway, Enoch was named chairman of the newly created history department. He served in that capacity until 1964.

During his tenure, Mitchell taught a number of courses but is best remembered for his Tennessee history course. He had a conversational style in the classroom, and he peppered his lectures with lively anecdotes. His knowledge of and enthusiasm for local, state and southern history were remarkable. His Tennessee history course was so popular that an exceptionally high percentage of Memphis State students took it, and the university established a distinguished faculty award in his honor.

Professor Mitchell was more of a "hands-on" than an "ivory-tower" historian. He participated actively in a number of historical associations, but none more so than our local West Tennessee Historical Society. As one of the society's incorporating members in 1950, Mitchell frequently served as an officer on the society's board of trustees. Moreover, between 1957 and 1964, he often served as either editor of the *WTHS Papers* and/or as a member of its editorial board. He authored two articles for the *Papers*: one on General George W. Gordon and the KKK and a second on Nicholas M. Long, an important local theologian. More importantly, he coauthored (with Stanley J. Folmsbee and Robert E. Corlew) a four-volume history of Tennessee, which became the standard work in the field. A single-volume abridgment of this work later served as the standard college text for Tennessee history courses over several decades and through multiple editions.

Sources for Memphis-Area History

Professor Enoch L. Mitchell seems to be editing or grading from a relatively clear desk, but books and papers are piled in disarray on the windowsill behind him. *Courtesy of Special Collections, University of Memphis.*

Mitchell was active in local politics, serving a two-year term as president of the Memphis Public Affairs Forum. He spoke to civic and service groups throughout the city and sometimes engaged in public debate. He and his wife, Ara Reed Mitchell, were founders and operators of the Blue and Gray Bookstore near the Memphis State campus.

Within Memphis State, Professor Mitchell was at least a player in bureaucratic politics. He helped found and directed the university's highly successful J.P. Young Lecture Series in American History, which brought historians of national stature to the campus each year. He also worked in the alumni office and chaired the alumni placement bureau. He helped establish the division of adult education on the campus as well. Finally, he was a founder and the director of the Memphis State University Press between 1955 and 1965.

For all of his productivity, Mitchell's administrative efforts were not universally admired. Supporters saw him as having a firm hand at the helm; critics viewed that hand as a mailed fist. Relinquishing the department's chairmanship was not his idea. When Mitchell stepped down, he accepted a distinguished professor endowed research chair.

Although he remained lively, Professor Mitchell did not live long after leaving his chairmanship. He died at his home at Christmas 1965. He had just hosted a holiday open house for friends and colleagues from the university, and he passed away quietly during the night.

When the History Department transferred out of the Administration Building in 1971, it moved into what had been the Business Administration Building. The university had just renovated this building and, shortly after the move, renamed it. Enoch's son, navy lieutenant commander Allan R. Mitchell, spoke movingly of his father's life and career at the dedication of Enoch Mitchell Hall.

Professor James E. Roper

Rhodes Scholar and Our City's Foremost Expert on Its Early History

Professor James E. Roper was a "Rhodes Scholar" in at least four senses of that phrase. First, he did his undergraduate work at Southwestern, now Rhodes College. Second, he studied for two years and earned a degree at Oxford University (Exeter College) through the prestigious Cecil Rhodes scholarship program. After earning his master's degree at Yale, Jim returned to Southwestern/Rhodes to teach English literature there from 1954 until his retirement in 1989. Finally, he wrote a history of Rhodes College, *Southwestern at Memphis: 1948–1975.* So not only did Jim Roper love word play, but in his academic pursuits he also lived it.

For all of his love for and the fun he had with the English language and its literature, Roper became disillusioned with the growing superficiality of literary criticism. In part because of that, but also because he was a fifth-generation Memphian who saw clearly how his city's heritage was being ill used or ignored, he immersed himself in Memphis history. He became the area's foremost scholar on the span between early exploration and the mid-nineteenth century. Roper wrote a goodly number of articles on the early Mid-South, publishing in the *West Tennessee Historical Society Papers,* the *Tennessee Historical Quarterly,* the *Delta Review* and other journals. His work corrected numerous aspects of Memphis lore. He wrote substantively on the De Soto expedition, Fort San Fernando, the early American forts, Benjamin Fooy, Paddy Meagher and his Bell Tavern and Charles Alexandre Lesueur's drawings of 1820s Memphis. At his own expense, he researched such topics in the archives of Britain, France and Spain.

Roper's detailed and meticulous 1970 book, *The Founding of Memphis: 1818– 1820,* is a slender but complex study. Its title is somewhat misleading, since it contains a concise thirty-six-page account of the area's history and its principal

Sources for Memphis-Area History

Charles Lesueur's late 1820s sketch of the Memphis waterfront at high water is among the earliest images of a city that would grow to contain skyscrapers and more than 600,000 citizens. *Courtesy of Memphis and Shelby County Room, Memphis Public Library.*

players prior to 1818. Then, scene by scene, Roper dramatically depicts the origins of our city and county. The book's appendices are also very valuable; except for the petition requesting the creation of Shelby County in Appendix B. Presumably the Tennessee State Archives had misidentified that item.

Perhaps even more valuable for local history enthusiasts than his *Founding of Memphis* would be Roper's detailed commentary in the West Tennessee Historical Society's 1972 facsimile reprint of James D. Davis's *The History of the City of Memphis*. Davis's book is often considered the first "history" of Memphis, although it may be more fictional than factual. Most subsequent historians relied heavily on Davis as their main source for the city's early decades. Thus, the myths that he created were often repeated as factual and woven into the fabric of our heritage. Only Jim Roper's strongly documented research has corrected many of the numerous Davis misstatements of fact.

Professor Roper wrote two other books: *The Decline and Fall of the Gibbon*, a funfest of historical puns and limericks, and his history of Southwestern College. But Jim Roper also aided and supported our local heritage in numerous ways beyond his research and writing. He was an early local preservationist, working to save the Memphis and Charleston Railroad Depot and later serving on and chairing the Memphis Landmarks Commission. Moreover, he served for many years on the Shelby County Historical Commission and was a founding member and major force (president, 1968–

71) in the West Tennessee Historical Society. He played key roles in the city's sesquicentennial observances, lectured widely to local civic and service groups on our area's history and acted as Memphis-area consultant to the Public Broadcasting System and *World Book Encyclopedia*.

Finally, any conversation with Jim Roper was an education in itself. He was erudite in a host of areas. His resume shows that he attended Yale on a Sterling Fellowship, but his friends and colleagues would have described him as a "sterling fellow" in just about every other sense of that phrase as well.

Robert A. Sigafoos

Scholar, Economist, Historian

I met Dr. Robert A. Sigafoos on a Sunday afternoon in 1979, in the Nellie Angel Smith woman's residence hall at Memphis State University. We were violating neither the university's rules nor those of decorum at the time. The now defunct Memphis State University Press was hosting a book-launching party for Sigafoos's *Cotton Row to Beale Street: A Business History of Memphis*. Dr. Bob was in a receiving line, and I was among those queued up to meet the author, wring his palm and evaluate his magnum opus. The twenty-odd-dollar price tag was a significant outlay at that time for an underpaid public library employee. But *Cotton Row* was and is more than worth its price. In the decades since, I have given perhaps two dozen copies to various friends, associates and kinfolks. Nearly three decades later, it remains, in many respects, the most useful single-volume reference book on Memphis and Shelby County history. I made very extensive use of it for my own books, *Metropolis of the American Nile* and *Historic Shelby County*.

For many months after encountering Sigafoos and *Cotton Row*, I was among those helping provide him with reference service for a second book with a local history impact. *Absolutely, Positively Overnight: Wall Street's Darling Inside and Up Close* was an in-depth, freelance "biography" of Fred Smith's Federal Express Corporation. By the time it was published in 1983, Bob and I had become pretty good friends, and he let me interview him about the book for my *Historically Speaking* program on the library's cable television network. Bob still has a videotape of that program and refers to our televised conversation quite fondly. FedEx, of course, is one of the four great business-history success stories from the Memphis scene; the other three are Piggly Wiggly, Holiday Inn and AutoZone.

Sources for Memphis-Area History

Shelby County's 1910 courthouse, the state's largest and most expensive to that time, housed city and county administrations and courts. It also symbolized the might of Crump's political organization. *Courtesy of Shelby County Archives.*

In the early 1990s, when Memphis State dismantled its university press, Sigafoos got in touch with me about *Cotton Row*. The press was liquidating its inventory, and I happened to be president of the West Tennessee Historical Society at the time. The society had discretionary funds on hand, and, in furtherance of its mission, it bought all seventeen hundred remaining copies of Bob's book. In addition to keeping this valuable book available for purchase, its sales have repaid the society's investment several times over. Accordingly, *Cotton Row* has enriched the telling and interpretation of our local history and has also helped to finance the activities of the area's most productive local history group.

As of 2009, Sigafoos was living a very active retirement in Fayetteville, Arkansas. I sent him "tear sheets" of this little article and let him know how much local history buffs appreciate his ongoing contributions to our self-understanding. I told him that, given recent orders from our Cotton Museum, the society's remaining copies of *Cotton Row* are nearly gone. Of course, used copies will probably be available online in the foreseeable future.

Metropolis of the American Nile
and *Historic Shelby County*

Needing Outside Support to Publish Our Area's History

Immodest as it may seem to suggest here, probably the two best general narratives on the Memphis area's history are my own *Metropolis of the American Nile** and *Historic Shelby County*. This should not be the case, but major and medium-sized publishers rarely publish local histories these days. "Niche publishers" have done much to fill the resulting vacuum. In 1981–82, I simply blundered into writing the text and selecting and captioning the pictures for *Metropolis*. The West Tennessee Historical Society had contracted to partner with the now defunct Windsor Publications (Woodland Hills, California) to produce an illustrated history of our fair city. I gave myself a cram course in local history and, with a lot of help from Windsor's fine editors, muddled through, producing a much better manuscript than the circumstances would have indicated likely.

Windsor was one of several publishers at that time utilizing the production formula that had been employed by the Goodspeed Company in the late nineteenth century. Goodspeed had used brief personal biographies and etched portraits of prominent local figures to produce and sell county history books. Modern niche publishers do something similar, but they substitute

The West Tennessee Historical Society sponsored both editions of *Metropolis of the American Nile*. Although out of print, it is often called the best single-volume, narrative history of Memphis.

corporate profiles for the biographical sketches. By charging a fee for having one's company included in the book, publishers raise the money for operational and production expenses. By including corporate profiles, they also create a fertile market for the end product. With the second edition of *Metropolis*, for example, one sponsoring bank purchased six hundred copies of the book to offer as holiday gifts to its best customers.

A similar financing method was used by Historical Publishing Network (HPN), operating from San Antonio, Texas, for the creation of *Historic Shelby County*. The publisher approached several local heritage institutions prior to engaging the West Tennessee Historical Society. Publisher, society and author struck mutually beneficial agreements, and the project went forward pretty smoothly. A professional sales campaign recruited corporate sponsors, who paid to have their entities' historical profiles included in the book. Thus, it was a four-way winning situation; plus, Memphis and Shelby County got a coffee-table book that would otherwise never have become a reality. This same business plan and method have been used to produce periodic "urban tapestry books" and even more specialized local history books. For example, in the spring of 2009, the Shelby County Bar Association produced such a book on the legal profession, and the Shelby County Medical Association has such a work on its healing profession underway.

The question then becomes: on balance, is this method or process a good thing? Well, it can be; but that is by no means a certainty. Despite relying on a local organization to help select an appropriate author, a publisher may contract with a person who is inept at research and/or writing. Even a competent historian may not take such a project very seriously and may dash off a sloppy text just to fulfill the terms of the contract. Perhaps the publisher's editorial support may fall below professional standards. Dozens of other things could go wrong.

Despite such perils, the fact remains that this profile-sponsored approach may currently be the only way to underwrite the production of much-needed local history. To reinforce that perspective, consider that the Goodspeed history of Shelby County was produced in 1887. Then, only when HPN tendered its business offer to WTHS was another general history of Shelby County created for local history enthusiasts. *Metropolis*, another subsidized coffee-table book, has been through two editions, sold more than ten thousand copies and has been out of print for about a decade. The book's staying power to date suggests that another edition is probably warranted, but it may well take an outside company's sales campaign and corporate sponsorships to make its republication economically feasible.

According to former acquisitions librarian Alice Ferris, for a good number of years Metropolis was the most frequently stolen and replaced title in the Memphis Public Library system.

A Lot of Good Local History
Never Gets Published

For various reasons, I occasionally receive copies of local history manuscripts, many of which may never get published. Often, these are good studies of interesting topics and probably merit publication. They range from very brief to book-length studies. Some are academic papers, including theses and dissertations. (Generating an academic treatise is sometimes grimly referred to as "digging up bones from one graveyard only to bury them in another.") Other such histories are researched and written out of pure passion for a topic. Some of these studies do eventually get published in local history journals. However, there are very few local organs for book publishing, especially since we lost St. Luke's Press and Memphis State University Press. If they can afford it, local writers may self-publish their books. Others simply make photocopies available to local repositories and/or to other local history enthusiasts. Over recent decades, I have accumulated several dozen high-quality manuscripts.

Some of my close colleagues are published writers but have not yet gotten their favorite stories published. For instance, Judge John B. Getz's most prized study is his "History of St. Brigid's [Catholic] Church." He has lovingly chronicled the story of this North Memphis Irish working-class parish from its 1870 founding to its 1938 demise. The abrupt closing of St. Brigid's marks a poignant instance in our city's shifting demographics. St. Mary's, Sacred Heart, Holy Names and Little Flower parishes absorbed St. Brigid's congregation. Its parish buildings were used for warehousing until they were razed in 1961. St. Brigid's name, though, has recently reappeared, honoring a new church in Germantown.

Dr. David Bowman, academician, community activist and retired journalist, might best like to see his "Memphis and the Politics of Development" published and widely circulated. In it, David reviews conflicts regarding high-profile land development cases from early urban renewal to the creation of the Mud Island theme park. He effectively argues that much of our development has been at odds with the broader public good. At times, such development has either "ripped off" public assets to the benefit of a few, or it has used public funds for boondoggles that never delivered the

St. Brigid's Parish served North Memphis Catholics from 1870 to 1938. Its school, convent and church were familiar landmarks at the corner of Third and Overton, near St. Joseph's Hospital. *Courtesy of Judge John B. Getz.*

expected public benefits. Bowman's study needs to be updated to include the Pyramid, the FedEx Forum, the RDC's Public Promenade project and the plan to run a light rail line from the airport to downtown. David's "Politics" manuscript vividly illustrates George Santayana's maxim that those who don't "remember the mistakes of the past are condemned to repeat them."

Perhaps best loved in my trove of unpublished manuscripts is John C. Rea's history of "The Street Railways of Memphis." For many years, John passionately and painstakingly researched, wrote, edited and photo-documented his manuscript. He covered the topic from its mule-drawn omnibus cars of 1859 to the last trolley run in 1947. John centered his life on this work. Had he lived, he would likely have seen it through to publication. Before he could publish, however, John's cancer resurfaced and he died. Hoping to get John's study published posthumously, his heirs lent his final text and photographs to a friend. The latter failed to get John's manuscript published and did not, perhaps could not, return it to the family. Thus, Rea's final treatment of the Memphis trolley system, with its profound effects on our city's geographical expansion and its demographic changes, may be forever lost to us.

There are numerous other unpublished nuggets of Memphis history. Mike Freeman, coauthor of an Elvis Presley book, found no publisher for his master's thesis treatment of Clarence Saunders and Piggly Wiggly. Likewise, Wylie McClallen's detailed treatment of Clarence Saunders's Memphis Tigers professional football team has only been published in a greatly abridged form in *Memphis Magazine*. Jonathan Smith, no longer a Shelby County resident, has written the fullest account yet of Bartlett, Tennessee's history.

My personal inventory of unpublished manuscripts may be impressive, but it's hardly all-inclusive. My point here is that those of us who love our history and are diligent in pursuing it need to help find ways to ensure that more "good stuff" gets published. We also need to find ways to show our appreciation for the knowledge and insights that local historians shed on our past.

Real People

TV Interviews with Bill Waters

In November 2007, WKNO producer Susan Shelton invited me to videotape an interview on the station's *Real People with Bill Waters* program. 'KNO searches out, engages and interviews persons perceived as making some sort of difference in our broader community. Bill interviews a fantastic variety of local folks on widely divergent topics. As a proponent of (or propagandist for) our area's history, I was delighted to participate.

Naturally, Bill asked me questions about unique aspects of local history, about research and writing history and about working with high school boys in the domain of the arcane. On the local history topics, we reviewed the roles of the West Tennessee Historical Society and the availability of Paul Coppock's classic books on Memphis history. Bill's pleasant and conversational interview included one pithy question that I had not anticipated.

He asked whether any of our Memphis University School alumni have entered and/or distinguished themselves in the field of history. Coincidental to the timing of our interview, local media were hyping an MUS alumnus named Hampton Sides and his new and highly acclaimed book, *Blood and Thunder*. Sides, in town for a book signing and perhaps the Southern Festival of Books, was never one of my students, but we are casually acquainted and I take joy in his achievements. His earlier major work, *Ghost Soldiers*, told the story of a daring rescue of American prisoners of war in the Philippines

WKNO-TV's *Real People* host Bill Waters converses on air with local historian and author John Harkins about the latter's teaching, writing and work with the West Tennessee Historical Society. *Courtesy of WKNO Television Station.*

near the end of World War II. A *New York Times* bestseller, this work was later adapted as a documentary on the History Channel. Ultimately, it became a critically acclaimed, big-screen (docudrama) movie. After the publication of *Ghost Soldiers* but before the making of the movie, Sides came back to MUS and told our students of his experiences in the world of writing and the zaniness of actually getting a movie into production. His responses during the question and answer session were perhaps more riveting than his prepared remarks.

Of course, MUS has graduated other young men who have become highly regarded academic (rather than popular) historians, and the school is equally proud of their achievements. It is difficult, however, for either our distinguished scholars or our local history to garner attention remotely akin to bestsellers or major motion pictures. I look forward to reading *Blood and Thunder* and to learning a good bit more about the Navajos' resistance to Kit Carson and America's westward expansion.

Popularizing Local History

Willy Bearden

William Bearden is passionate about storytelling, Mid-South history and his work. Two years ago, I was not even casually acquainted with this Memphis filmmaker and videographer. I did own and had read one of his books, and I had seen most of his documentary television productions on Memphis history. Even so, I did not connect them to each other and did not even have a face to put with his name.

Over the last year, however, Willy has become one of my local history heroes. He writes, produces, directs and edits many sorts of videos. A list of his commercial clients reads like a who's who of Mid-South commercial and cultural entities. He also produces and records meetings, conventions and live events at regional, national and international levels. A child of the Mississippi Delta, Willy is devoted to its history and culture, especially its musical traditions. Of course, Delta soul music is a vital element of Memphis culture.

Perhaps more important for Memphis history buffs, Bearden has produced and made available for television airing local and regional history videos. These include *Overton Park: A Century of Change*; *Elmwood: Reflections of Memphis*; *Playing for a Piece of the Door: A History of Memphis Garage Bands*; and, most recently, *The History of Cotton*. He has authored three history books: *Overton Park*; *Cotton: From Southern Fields to the Memphis Market*; and *Memphis Blues: Birthplace of a Music Tradition*. Usually premiering on PBS affiliate WKNO, Bearden's television documentaries also get repeated airings on WYPL TV-18 (the local library channel). Bearden's creative work has generated both critical and popular acclaim in all of its venues. His work has earned numerous honors, including Telly, Best of Broadcast and Aegis Awards.

Willy's artistic and historical contributions are not limited to the creative arts. He has also given service to numerous boards, workshops and symposia. I have attended all three University of Memphis Delta symposia and found his portions of the programs as entertaining as they were informative. Moreover, the program that he delivered to the West Tennessee Historical Society in the spring of 2006 captivated his audience completely (despite the fact that our AV equipment could not be accessed and he "winged" his presentation without any visual support).

Bearden is a masterful and spellbinding storyteller. He uses state-of-the-art techniques to interpret and popularize our area's history for people

Willy Bearden is likely reaching more mid-southerners with his popular videos on our area's history than any other individual working in local history. Bearden has produced excellent pictorial books and video programs documenting the histories of Overton Park, cotton and blues music. *Courtesy of the William Bearden Co.*

who might never make the effort to read about the same topics. His stories resonate with his audiences, and they inspire us to learn and to enjoy our local history beyond any other resource currently available. Finally, Willy's mission is to educate. He does much of his educational work gratis and inspires others to do likewise.

Margot Stern Strom

Former Memphian Who Literally Started Something Great

During the 1980s, the Memphis Convention and Visitors' Bureau made extensive use of a catchy, community-promoting jingle urging that we "Start something great in Memphis, where great things always start." This campaign publicized a number of the great things that have had their origins in our fair city but omitted one that had its roots in Memphis but actually got started in Brookline, Massachusetts. I refer to an educational program called

Facing History and Ourselves (FHAO). It was co-founded by Margot Stern Strom, who has been its executive director since its inception. Margot's inspiration for creating and promoting a different approach to history came out of her childhood experiences, growing up in the Jim Crow culture of pre-1960s Memphis. This atmosphere meant much more than just separate bus seating, restrooms and water fountains. Such sanctioned discrimination was merely symbolic of harder divisions across racial lines, with almost everything in the culture emphasizing "otherness" and calculated to reinforce racial stereotypes and caricatures. Margot's exposure to deeply rooted racism was more than tempered by her own family's values of inclusion and striving for understanding across racial lines. All Memphians of a certain age can remember that there were often close, virtually familial and close individual attachments across racial lines, but these did not preclude each race from broadly viewing the other race with suspicion and mistrust, or even condescension and contempt.

In 1976, Margot taught in Brookline's Runkle School and studied moral development at Harvard. Attending a major conference on the Holocaust changed her life. With her enhanced perceptions, she developed lessons and resources that focus on issues of individual responsibility and ethical decision-making for America's youth. She took her program of examining ourselves, plus the failures of various democracies, to the next level. Her concepts now make up an internationally acclaimed and implemented FHAO approach to the study of group relations, including genocides. They explore difficult problems involving memory, legacies and judgment. Her program concludes by stressing the inseparable link between history and ethics and our responsibility for protecting and promoting America's highest ideals.

Margot's hometown of Memphis has been a center for implementing FHAO programs. Under the leadership of Rachel Shankman, the local program has held hundreds of seminars and workshops and is educating thousands of our region's teachers in FHAO's methods for communicating the values of democracy, human dignity and justice. Although FHAO did not technically begin in Memphis, its connection has built a strong presence in our city. The national office is headquartered in Brookline, and the Memphis regional office is on the Christian Brothers University campus. FHAO's website can be accessed at www.facinghistory.org.

Heroes in Our History?

Among the perquisites of teaching at Memphis University School is enjoying the quality and variety of assembly programs. Occasionally, our speakers are personalities of national or even international stature. Some of these come in for annual endowed lecture series, like our Metcalf Symposium. Others are serendipitous opportunities that arise through our faculty's collegial connections. The latter was the case when, at the behest of history teacher Eric Berman, Dr. Peter H. Gibbon came in late January to speak to the MUS community (and at several other Memphis schools). His topic was "Heroes in America."

Following an impressive career in academics and school administration, Dr. Gibbon spent ten years researching and writing the book *A Call to Heroism: Renewing America's Vision of Greatness.* Since his book's publication, Gibbon has been touring our nation and doing precisely what the subtitle of his book advocates. He first lectures on heroism and then holds discussions with students and faculty, analyzing and exploring the many facets of what is heroic and why. He notes that since the 1960s, we have been living in an anti-heroic age, one awash with cynicism, obsessive attention to sex and celebrities and disdain for political and military figures. Noting further that America has "come to define the person by the flaw," individuals like Christopher Columbus, Thomas Jefferson and Albert Einstein have been booted out of America's pantheon of heroes. In fact, the very concept of heroism has become intellectually and socially unfashionable, even taboo, in many circles.

Admitting that consensus on what defines a "hero" is difficult to reach and that subjectivity will always have its role, Gibbon encourages his audiences to reflect on their personal heroes, past and present. Most of us seem to agree that heroes are persons who have overcome adversity in some extraordinary way. Whether through a single act of courage, like Tom Lee saving survivors of a capsized Mississippi riverboat, or the sustained activities of Mother Teresa ministering to the lepers of Calcutta, as in other areas, we usually recognize the real thing when we encounter it.

Dr. Gibbon had done some homework before coming to Memphis. He knew of Ida B. Wells's work to stop lynching here and of the city's controversy over keeping the names of its Confederate-motif public parks. He visited the Civil Rights Museum and toured Historic Elmwood Cemetery and Shiloh National Military Park before leaving our area. He was impressed with what he found here, and he hopes to return soon, to bring his message to additional local schools and to learn more about Memphis-area heroes.

Prominent educator and author Peter Gibbon is on a mission to restore the role of heroism to his countrymen's sense of American history. He convinced his audience at MUS. *Courtesy of Professor Peter Gibbon.*

MUS students responded enthusiastically to Dr. Gibbon's lecture. More important, many of them gave up free class periods later that day to participate in one or more of his hour-long student forums. Attendance was even strong during the last period of the week, during which students who do not have classes or labs are permitted to leave campus. The following Monday, students in each of my classes wanted to resume Friday's discussions. Gibbon's riveting Socratic exchanges with our young men struck a chord with them. His work with them epitomizes some of the best elements that a traditional liberal arts education should provide. Observing the quality of our students' interaction proved a joy to Dr. Gibbon and to MUS teachers. It exemplified the nobility of our profession. Well done, Peter Gibbon! Thank you for your gift to America's youth and to their teachers.

Go online to www.heroesinamerica.org to learn more about Peter Gibbon and the importance of heroism in our history or to contact Dr. Gibbon.

PART II

Frontier Days and Nineteenth-Century Social History

Before Memphis Was Here

Spanish and American Forts on the Fourth Chickasaw Bluff

We Memphians usually celebrate 1819 as the date of our city's founding and Andrew Jackson, John Overton and James Winchester as its founders. Such commemorations are inaccurate. There has been recorded continuous occupancy of the Fourth Chickasaw Bluff since at least 1795. Thus, for a generation prior to 1819 there had been a small settlement here. This community just didn't start being called Memphis until about 1820.

After America's Revolutionary War, Spain and the United States both claimed most of present-day Kentucky, Tennessee, Alabama and Mississippi. Spain based its claim on having conquered British military posts in the lower Mississippi Valley and along the Gulf Coast. America based its claim on Britain having ceded to it lands that Britain no longer actually controlled. Initially, neither the United States nor Spain attempted to consolidate their claims to Trans-Appalachia. Following the French Revolution, and amid a series of diplomatic realignments, Spain did move to assert its control of the disputed area.

In May 1795, Spain sent troops under Manuel Gayoso de Lemos to acquire the Chickasaws' permission and then build a small stockade fort about where the Pyramid is now. Gayoso's men soon erected the fort and some outbuildings nearby. (See the maps on pages 49 and 112.) Gayoso named the fort San Fernando de las Barrancas as a tribute to Spain's Crown Prince Ferdinand. Upon Gayoso's departure, some of his Franco-Spanish troops occupied the fort for nearly two years. As these things happened in the Mississippi Valley, Spanish diplomats in Europe were negotiating

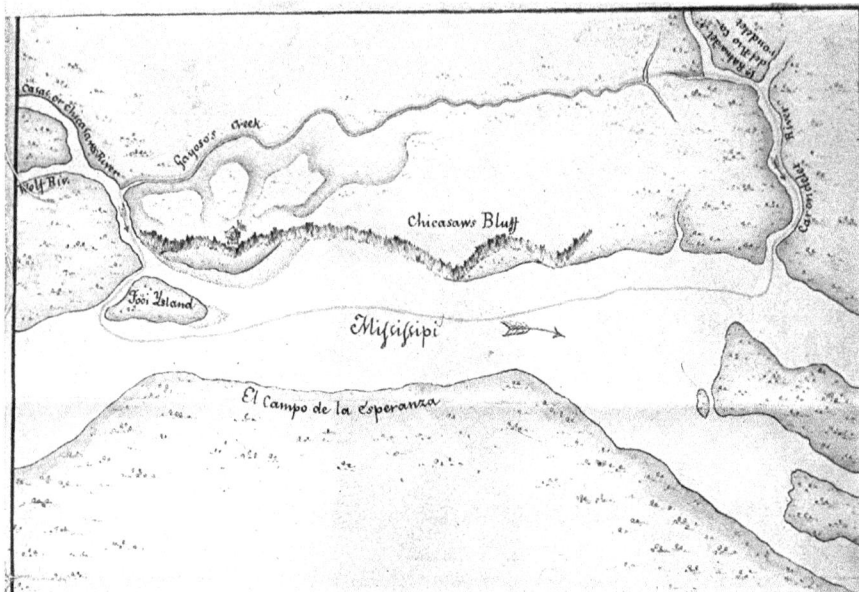

This 1795 Spanish map of the Fourth Chickasaw Bluff antedates the founding of Fort San Fernando de las Barrancas and the beginning of continuous European settlement of the Memphis area. *Courtesy of the Spanish National Archives, Madrid.*

Frontier Days and Nineteenth-Century Social History

Front Street, circa 1910, was the city's primary economic artery. Cotton businesses lined the east side of the street, with the Cossitt Library and the U.S. Customhouse standing opposite. *Courtesy of Special Collections, University of Memphis.*

Pinckney's Treaty, by which they renounced their claims to all of eastern Trans-Appalachia above the thirty-first parallel.

After Spain ceded its territorial claims to America and withdrew its small garrison across the Mississippi River, the U.S. Army occupied the bluff area and ultimately established two posts, Fort Adams (which was later called Fort Pike) and Fort Pickering, farther south atop the bluff. American commandants at those forts included legendary explorer Meriwether Lewis, Zebulon Pike (father of another famous explorer) and Zachary Taylor (who later became America's twelfth president). Following the 1803 Louisiana Purchase, the Mississippi River was no longer an international boundary, and the American army scaled back and then withdrew its presence. However, a government-operated trading post or "factory" continued to function on the site for about another decade. Various European-American settlers continued to live close to the forts and factory until the Chickasaw Cession officially opened West Tennessee to settlement in 1819.

Some of the same families reported as being on hand at the arrival of American troops in 1797 were still living here when the proprietors had the city's streets laid out. Their names appear on the petition to the Tennessee legislature for the creation of Shelby County. Among those present under the Spanish and still here in 1819 were Kenneth Ferguson, John Measle and Patrick Meagher, who later owned and operated the legendary Bell Tavern.

Manuel Gayoso de Lemos commanded the Spanish troops who built the Fort San Fernando de las Barrancas settlement. It stood where the Wolf River entered the Mississippi. *Courtesy of Special Collections, University of Memphis.*

(Spellings of early settlers' names vary widely in documents of the times.) These were the pioneers who actually created and shaped the community that became early Memphis. These unsung, plain folk, rather than the absentee proprietors (Jackson, Overton and Winchester), should properly be celebrated as our city's founders.

For detailed information on the Spanish fort, see "Fort San Fernando de las Barrancas: An Essay Review" by John E. Harkins and Georgia S. Harkins in the *West Tennessee Historical Papers* (1996). For more information on our American forts, see James E. Roper's "Fort Adams and Fort Pickering" in the *West Tennessee Historical Society Papers* (1970). For information about local historical organizations, contact the Linc Department at the Public Library at (901) 415-2700 or search online at www.memphislibrary.org.

A Pioneer's Perceptions of Shelby County and Its Indians in the 1820s

In my recent writing of *Historic Shelby County*, I quote extensively from our county's 1874–75 *Old Folks Record*. An article written by early settler J.J.

Native Americans, mainly the Chickasaws and the Choctaws, lived farther south and did not present much danger to West Tennesseans. Many frontiersmen, however, feared Indians as potentially hostile. *Courtesy of Special Collections, University of Memphis.*

Rawlings, nephew of pioneer Memphian Isaac Rawlings, describes his recollections of trading with local Indians in the 1820s:

> *The Indians came in caravans, with their ponies well packed with cow-hides, deerskins, beaver, bear and otter, and an innumerable quantity of coon-skins, which were exchanged for blankets, striped domestics (cloth yard-goods), tobacco, whisky, &c.* [No] *Railroads, nor even country roads were known in that day.* They [Indians] *traveled a path in single file through the wilderness.*
>
> *In writing about a nation or tribes that have no* [written] *history, we can only write from personal observation. The Chickasaws and Choctaws, in their primeval condition, were a happy set in their way. Their wants were but few, and a support was easily made. Nature had bountifully provided for them—the country abounded in game, such as they thought the Great Spirit had provided especially for their use. It was part of their means to supply their families with meat.*
>
> *When they* [the braves] *started hunting they provided themselves with a little bag of "tomfuller," as they called it. It was parched corn, gritted*

into meal—a spoonful or two put into a tin cup, with a little sugar and water, made a very palatable beverage. A small bag, that they could stick under their belt[s], would last them a week.

By their tribal laws, they were entitled to as many wives as they could support. Good hunters generally had three or four wives. It was their business to do the housework and cultivate ground sufficient for the support of the family. Their cultivated patches were generally small and their products principally consisted of pumpkins, corn, beans, potatoes, with a small orchard consisting of peaches and plums; the women got along happily together—hardly ever disagreed; the men supplied them with meat, such as bear, venison, turkey, &c. There was nothing to interrupt their happiness as they said, until they became acquainted with white men.

Although, as a nation, they were treacherous and thievish, some were high-minded and honorable, proud and remarkably fond of dress. There is a great similarity of dress pertaining to all the different tribes of Indians. The leggings and moccasins they donned were manufactured by themselves. They dressed in the skin of a deer, cut out the leggings in proper shape and sewed up with the sinews taken from the deer. In the same way were made the moccasins worn upon their feet—the [upper] body was always covered by a blanket.

There were among them some very ingenious workmen in brass and silver. Large silver ear-rings were worn in the ears and nose, and silver bands around their wrists. Some of these ornaments were curiously carved in the shape of eagles, owls, serpents, &c.

Here is a follow-up extract from Rawlings, published in the *Old Folks Record* and entitled "The Aborigines of the County: the Chickasaws and Choctaws":

When these people [the Chickasaws and Choctaws] were first discovered, they were complete children of nature; they knew nothing about the arts and sciences of more civilized countries. Their own native ingenuity invented the bow and arrow, which they used with great precision. They would hit a copper cent oftener than miss it at thirty or forty paces. When using the bow for hunting large game they used a bearded [barbed] arrow, and when once struck into a bear or deer it could not be pulled out, so they would capture the game with their dogs, of which they always had innumerable quantities.

Rawlings then describes their adaptation to a changing world:

During the time these vast improvements were going on, Civilization was doing its work. They were becoming surrounded by a different class of people; the encroachments were daily increasing. They at first resisted these encroachments of the whites—but to no purpose; it was destined to accomplish its work; the progress of one nation was the destruction of another. They could not readily account for the effects that circumstances were producing. Game of all kinds was gradually disappearing; their hunting grounds were contracted. They would ask among themselves— "Why is it that deer are so scarce in the hills? Why is it that [there are] no bear in the jungles? What has become of the beaver and otter that once abounded in our streams?" Exclaiming also: "Our country is changing; it is fast becoming unfit for our habitation."

Ah, and changed it has! You can imagine a poor lonely squaw, thinly dressed, barefooted, on a cold, bleak evening, with her little "pushcush" (a baby) upon her back, (probably not a fortnight old), treading a lonely path about two feet wide, hunting the camp-fire that the men have gone ahead to prepare. That camp-fire was on this bluff, where now stands large three

Front Street, the city's face in 1845, looked like a western town, not a southern city entering an economic and construction boom era. Railroads would soon hasten that expansion. *Courtesy of Memphis and Shelby County Room, Memphis Public Library.*

and four story brick houses, groaning under the weight of supplies for a civilized people. Near by that little two [foot] path now runs a locomotive at twenty miles an hour; mysterious change that has occurred in my own time, and under my personal observation.

Civilization was the bane of these poor people. They had discovered its effects before they consented to move. The introduction of whisky at once carried many a one to another country—where they had no use for the bow and arrow—the old flint-lock, nor the percussion cap.

Early impressions are said to be the most lasting. When but [as] a boy I was intimately associated with those people for five years. I had partially learned their language, studied their character, and become possessed in their favor. Their move to the West I think was best for them, and I hope they [are] doing well and prospering as a nation.

Writing later for the *Old Folks Record*, Rawlings relates two of his early Memphis experiences:

When I first landed on this bluff, my preceptor had in his employ an interpreter by the name of Measels—Jack Measels. He was a half-breed Cherokee, but [also] spoke the Chickasaw and Choctaw languages. Jack was a very stout robust man and weighed about two hundred pounds. He frequently boasted about his aquatic performances and proposed to bet one hundred dollars that he could swim the Mississippi River at high tide. The boys soon made up the hundred dollars, though Jack had nothing to put up against it. When the river became very full, the time arrived for Jack to win or lose his bet. He crossed the river in a skiff, jumped off at Foy's Point (the present railroad landing) and landed at Fort Pickering, thus winning the bet and pocketing the hundred dollars—more money than he ever had had at one time before. I have never known the feat to be repeated.

In 1824, while at breakfast one Sunday morning, I was aroused by a noise, whooping, hallooing, &c. I ran out to see what was the matter. A huge bear was making his way through town, and all the boys, black and white, dogs and terriers were after him. Old Paddy Meagher lived in a log house on the bluff. Old Paddy had two awful curs, that he kept chained in the day and turned loose at night, much to the terror of us boys who gave his premises a wide berth after [dark]. Old Paddy thought his two dogs could capture anything in the shape of an animal.

As the bear approached his house he turned loose his dogs. They had not learned the strategy of fighting a bear and naturally they seized him by the throat and ears. With one lick of his paw the bear cut one nearly in *two, killing him immediately and wounded the other so badly that he died in a few days.* [This was] *much to the chagrin of old Paddy, but very gratifying to us boys, who thought we could now pay an evenings visit to his daughter Sally, unmolested by those infernal dogs.*

The bear made his way through town, and just at the water's edge, Henry James shot him in the head with a rifle. He was butchered and divided out among the people of the village. All had bear [meat] *enough and to spare.*

The Old Paddy Meagher (pronounced Marr) to whom Rawlings refers was arguably the first Memphian. He was at the bluff during the Revolutionary War, when the Spanish and American forts occupied the site and when the proprietors gave him land in 1819. Paddy sold supplies to riverboats from his store atop the bluff before the Chickasaw Cession. Thereafter, he was "the genial host" of the Bell Tavern. Given the date Rawlings affixes to his tale, the Bell was likely the log structure to which he refers. In Professor James Roper's *Founding of Memphis*, his commentary on James Davis's *History of Memphis* and in several articles appearing in the *WTHS Papers*, Roper revises many myths related to Paddy Meagher and the Bell Tavern. Memphis lost one of its most colorful characters when Meagher died shortly after the events that Rawlings describes above.

Shelby County Cotton and the Great Crystal Palace Exhibition of 1851

Shelby County's phenomenal population growth from about 2,500 in 1820 to nearly 300,000 persons forty years later was driven by the clearing of its land and its citizens' production of cotton. Much of northeast Shelby County was particularly fertile, and it produced some of the world's finest upland or short-staple cotton. Dr. Samuel Bond moved into this area in 1831 and became one of its major planters within a short time. In the late 1840s, he built a stately three-story, Greek revival home, which he called "the Avenue." This beautiful home's name was later changed to Cedar Hall, for the avenue of cedar trees leading to its entry. The nearby railroad (first the Memphis and Ohio, later the Louisville and Nashville) stop was first named Bond's Station, but it was later changed to Ellendale. Bond's plantation encompassed more than seven hundred acres in the 1850s, when he mortgaged it in order to develop lands in Louisiana.

In the mid-1840s, Bond had given up his medical practice to be a full-time planter. He must have been good at growing cotton, for his entry in

THE WEST TENNESSEE HISTORICAL SOCIETY
PAPERS

VOLUME XLI 1987

Dr. Samuel Bond's Shelby County–grown cotton won the medal for short-staple cotton at London's Crystal Palace Exhibition (in essence the first world's fair) in 1851. *Courtesy of West Tennessee Historical Society.*

London's Great Crystal Palace Exposition of 1851 took the medal for its category. This exhibition, organized to demonstrate and celebrate Britain's industrial superiority, was Western Civilization's first "world's fair." Thus, Shelby County had a claim to producing the finest cotton in the world at that time. Cotton, of course, was the mainstay of Britain's textile industry at this time, and textiles drove Britain's Industrial Revolution.

In the late twentieth century, Mrs. Virginia Bond-Montgomery donated Dr. Bond's Crystal Palace Medal to the Memphis Brooks Museum of Art. Thereafter, Dr. Marius Carriere presented a fairly detailed rendering of Samuel Bond's achievement as the cover story in the 1987 issue of the *West Tennessee Historical Society Papers*. Moreover, local historian Perre Magness gives a more detailed account of Samuel Bond and Cedar Hall in the Junior League's 1983 coffee-table book, *Good Abode*.

Thus, there is a good deal of Shelby County's wonderful nineteenth-century history all around us, if we only take the time and trouble to find it. Some of these stories will be available when my own *Historic Shelby County* appears later this year.

A Slave's Perspective on
Plantation Life Hereabouts

A little more than two years ago, the West Tennessee Historical Society agreed to partner with the Historical Publishing Network out of San Antonio, Texas, in the creation of an illustrated history of Shelby County. The need for such a work was obvious. The last broad-based history of Shelby County had been published in 1887, 120 years ago! Many notable things have happened hereabouts since then, and the Goodspeed version of Shelby's history was neither truly comprehensive nor very well researched and written.

I signed on to research and write the history and to choose and caption its images. I had learned a good bit about county history during my six years as Memphis/Shelby County archivist and in my research for *Metropolis of the American Nile*. In addition, I had been squirreling away news clippings and

Backbreaking toil was the lot of most rural African Americans prior to World War II in the Mid-South. Their labor supplied much of the world with the miracle fiber cotton. *Courtesy of Memphis and Shelby County Room, Memphis Public Library.*

photocopies on county history since before I left archival work in 1985. In addition, I had numerous, well-informed local history contacts to rely on. Although I had to do a considerable amount of additional research, it was nothing like starting from scratch. Finally, local historians have published a number of valuable studies on various aspects of Shelby County over the last several decades. Thus, I was hooked!

Perhaps the most exciting and fortunate of my research experiences was when Shelby County archivist John Dougan directed me to a memoir written by a former Shelby County slave named Louis Hughes. Published in the late 1890s and facsimile reprinted in the 1960s, the book's full title is *Thirty Years a Slave: From Bondage to Freedom, The Institution of Slavery as Seen on the Plantation and in the Home of the Planter.* It is interesting purely as an autobiographical narrative, but, more important for me, it describes in considerable detail how Mid-South cotton plantations operated in the 1840s and '50s. Information from this narrative forms the basis for chapter four of *Historic Shelby County.*

Louis's story takes him from his early life near Charlottesville, Virginia; describes his sale and teenage trek to Pontotoc, Mississippi; reviews his experiences as a house servant on a cotton plantation there; and relates his household's relocation to a grand home near the Memphis and Charleston Railroad, just outside of Memphis. Although Louis's prospective hardly fits the "moonlight and magnolias" view of the antebellum South, it is singularly bereft of bitterness or rancor. Hughes tried to escape upriver to Canada on two occasions. After his second failure, his owner personally beat him severely. Louis describes, almost clinically, mistreatment, as well as some positive aspects of his life under slavery. Ultimately, in the aftermath of the Civil War, Louis, his wife and his sister-in-law escaped from the plantation and moved north. They found portions of their respective families once they lived above the Ohio River.

Thirty years later, Louis published his recollections. It is uncertain whether he actually penned the story or it was "as told to" an accomplished writer. The Hughes account seems forthright and has historical verisimilitude as reflected in its internal evidence. I have since encountered small additional pieces of historical evidence that help to substantiate peripheral parts of his memoir. The text of the Hughes memoir can be found and accessed online at http://docsouth.unc.edu/fpn/hughes/menu.html. Thanks again to John Dougan and Stoy Bailey for leading me to this very valuable source.

"The Mackerel Brigade"

Criminal Youth Gangs in 1860s and '70s Memphis

The term *Mackerel Brigades* referred to juvenile street gangs that sprang up in 1860s Memphis. In the early 1980s, Mr. Robert Livingston Jr. first told me about the Mackerels. He has generously shared his voluminous research notes and photocopied materials with me. I was primarily interested in the Mackerels as potentially a part of our city's Irish-American history.

The seeds of the Mackerels were discernable in Memphis by 1863. Social stresses brought on by the Civil War and military occupation made these urchins more numerous and conspicuous. A breakdown of traditional authority, a decline of ethical and social standards, familial dislocations, a rise of rampant opportunism and vigilantism on the part of local groups like the Klan all doubtlessly exacerbated the rise of juvenile crime. By 1863, groups of wayward boys were getting attention in the newspapers, which originally identified them as "newsboys." (In her *Recollections of 92 Years*, Elizabeth Avery Meriwether refers to the Mackerels stealing and reselling newspapers.) Within three years, the local papers began collectively and consistently calling such gangs "Mackerel Brigades." The actual origin of the name is long and complicated, but it had absolutely no relationship to the city's Irish community or to anti-Catholic bigotry, as I had once supposed.

Problems with indigenous, troublemaking waifs intensified markedly when boys started arriving by boat from upriver. In March 1865, the *Memphis Bulletin* noted that over twenty such boys had arrived in Memphis in a mere fortnight. Ranging in age from eight to fifteen, the paper described them as dirty, ragged and audacious vagrants, hanging out in gangs numbering from four to eight. Initially, according to Livingston, the local gangs did not "generally associate with [the newcomer] thieves." Soon thereafter, however, the two sets of gangs merged under the leadership of one Thomas Porter. Tom had first come to public notice in May 1863, when he and three confederates stole $5,400 from a major commercial house during business hours. A city detective named Johnson quickly tracked the miscreants down and recovered the money.

Generally, the Mackerels stole clothes, food, footwear, booze, tobacco, candy, cotton and other cargo off the levee. Porter continued to be the notorious leader of the Mackerels until his final break-in in March 1868. Apprehended in the act, Tom and two confederates were taken to the police station, where Porter tried to make a run for freedom. When he ignored the pursuing officers' commands to halt, one of the policemen shot Tom, killing

Well into the twentieth century, making moonshine whiskey remained a serious problem in Shelby County. Local officials destroyed stills and confiscated both the machinery and the "white lightening." *Courtesy of Shelby County Archives.*

the nineteen-year-old kingpin. Since Porter had a horrendous reputation, including reputedly having murdered a Union soldier during the war, the *Avalanche* article on the young desperado's end concludes that the police had rendered the community a good service in killing him.

Jake Ackerman, another migrant into Memphis, briefly succeeded Porter as the recognized leader of the Mackerels. Ackerman's criminal actions appeared frequently in the newspapers between 1867 and 1869. Then he left town and did not return until 1873, at which time his being "drummed out of town" again made local headlines. Ackerman, too, ultimately met a violent end in Memphis. After decades of criminal acts across much of the nation, Jake returned again to Memphis in 1890. There, his wife, Lizzie, had him arrested for wife beating and then shot him to death in a Memphis courtroom before he could be tried. Although convicted, Lizzie served very little time for her crime.

Much less is known of other individual Mackerels, but the papers give a good bit of general information. In October 1867, Mayor Lofland estimated that there were between two and three hundred gamins in Memphis, many of whom were Mackerels. Memphis newspapers also referred (perhaps inaccurately) to a few female and freed black urchins as Mackerels. In March 1868, the police station released thirty-nine juvenile detainees at one time, simply because the city could not afford to feed them.

Efforts were made to rehabilitate some of the boys, but generally to no avail. Repeat juvenile offenders were generally tried as adults in criminal courts. Usually they could not pay their fines and, thus, had to serve time on the chain gang. The longest juvenile sentence mentioned in the papers was 103 days. The boys' confinement with hardened adult criminals seemed to have reinforced their criminal behaviors.

Although there are occasional references to Memphis Mackerels in 1870s newspapers, their importance declined notably with Porter's death and Ackerman's exile. There is also some evidence that Chief Phil R. Athy's leadership on the police department cut down on criminal behavior citywide. Moreover, the 1869 end of Reconstruction locally and the reestablishment of "home rule" by traditional local elites also seemed to have generally curbed lawlessness, including much juvenile crime.

An Unsung Hero of the Yellow Fever

Reverend Dennis A. Quinn

with coauthor John B. Getz

Perhaps the least celebrated hero of the disastrous Memphis yellow fever epidemics of the 1870s is Reverend Dennis A. Quinn. Ironically, he is the author of a book about heroes of that era.

In 1867, at age twenty-one, Dennis Quinn emigrated from Ireland to the United States. After training at several American Catholic seminaries, he was ordained in 1871. Although assigned to shepherd Catholic missions in eastern Arkansas, he was domiciled closer to his flocks at the recently founded St. Brigid's Church in Memphis.

When the yellow fever epidemic of 1873 struck Memphis, St. Brigid's was at the geographical heart of the plague. At deadly peril, young Father Quinn ministered to the spiritual and corporal needs of the stricken throughout the course of the epidemic. Five local priests and more than eight hundred of St. Brigid's parishioners died before a killing frost finally ended the epidemic. After visiting his family in Ireland, Quinn continued to serve as assistant pastor at St. Brigid's and to service the missions in eastern

The St. Brigid complex. The Irish working-class parishioners of St. Brigid's Church accounted for nearly half of all the lives lost in the 1873 yellow fever epidemic. *Courtesy of Judge John B. Getz.*

Arkansas and in West Tennessee. During that time, he was responsible for the erection of small churches at Brinkley, Forrest City and Hopefield (all in eastern Arkansas).

Quinn was tending rural mission needs across the Mid-South when the even more disastrous epidemics of 1878 and 1879 struck. Thinking he was immune to the fever, since he had eluded its ravages in 1873, Quinn asked to be assigned to succor the stricken in Memphis. The bishop refused his request. Thus, although Quinn was in and out of Memphis during the two plagues—including visiting fever refugees at nearby Camp Father Matthew—he was not endangered to the extent that he had been in 1873.

In the fevers' aftermath, Father Quinn wished to be named pastor of St. Brigid's, but this request, too, was denied him. Instead, the bishop appointed him pastor of St. Patrick's Parish in Memphis, where he served only two years. Then, in the face of his generally declining health, Quinn took a leave of absence and journeyed again to Ireland to recuperate. During his absence, he was replaced at St. Patrick's. Soon after his return, he was reassigned to the diocese of Providence, Rhode Island. Still in frail health, he suffered at least two strokes, the second of which left him an invalid for the rest of his life. Unable to perform the rigorous duties of a

Frontier Days and Nineteenth-Century Social History

When the disastrous yellow fever epidemics of the 1870s struck Memphis, various relief groups set up refugee camps outside the city, giving a modicum of protection from the dread disease. *Courtesy of Special Collections, University of Memphis.*

parish priest, Quinn served in a series of three institutional chaplaincies between 1885 and 1909.

It was during these years that he wrote three books. His most enduring work is *Heroes and Heroines of the Memphis Yellow Fever Epidemics.* Reacting to John Keating's history of the city's yellow fever crises, Quinn wanted fuller and more accurate coverage of the Catholic clergy's role in combating the plague. He remedied Keating's omissions and told the story from a strongly Catholic vantage. *Heroes* quickly went through two printings and received considerable praise in Catholic circles, with one admirer proclaiming that he would rather have authored Quinn's *Heroes* "than wear the best miter [bishop's headdress] ever manufactured."

After thirty-eight years of priestly service, Dennis Quinn retired to Ireland in 1909. That same year, he penned his autobiography. There, despite frail health and disability, he lived until about 1927, the last year that his name appears in Ireland's *Catholic Directory.* Had Quinn been martyred combating the fever, he would not have lived to focus our city's attention on the faith, courage and sacrifices made by his co-religionists during the deadly plagues of the 1870s.

Coauthor and retired general sessions judge John B. Getz was the St. Peter's Catholic Church historian, and he researched and wrote widely on the Memphis Irish, the Catholic Church in Memphis and aspects of the legal profession in Shelby County.

PART III

Local Schools and Some of Their Products

High School Yearbooks and Class Reunions

My Christian Brothers High School (CBHS) class graduated fifty years ago, in May 1956. What a milestone! Our reunion committee is putting together its seventh reunion, contacting classmates and coaxing them to attend our gathering in mid-October. Some of these "boys" have been close since kindergarten. Others arrived much later, and some remained loners. Many have gone on to that most final of commencements. The ever-resourceful Nathan Pera has spearheaded most of our gatherings. Other reunion stalwarts have been and are: Eugene McDermott, Monte Stark, John Colton, John McCabe, Ed Hardwick, Irvin Schatz, Pat Arnoult and Bob Patterson. Reviewing the 1956 *Chronicle* refreshes and intensifies mixed memories of our salad days.

John Cohen and Murray Wagner co-edited the annual, and Bob Frank did the photography. Highlights from the book include class picks to the seniors' Hall of Fame. The seniors chose Ed Hardwick (Most Athletic), Marion Brown (Best Student), Andrew Battaile (Wittiest), Ronnie Bruno (Best Dressed), Jimmy Peternell (Most Musical), Billy Hartley (Friendliest), A.W. Karchmer (Most Likely to Succeed) and Eugene McDermott (Contributed Most to the Class). Within the broader culture, the boys' favorites included: Town & Country (Drive-In), *Rebel Without a Cause* (Movie), Notre Dame (College), St. Agnes (Girls' School), Stan Kenton (Orchestra) and James Dean and Kim Novak (Actors).

The class of '56 initiated student government, put on the play *Rehearsal for Death* and produced multiple issues of the *Maurelian* (newspaper). With a 5–1–1 record, our football team came in second in the city's prep league and furnished seven players on the All-Memphis Squad. The 1955–56 basketball

John Cohen, Murray Wagner (seated) and the 1956 *Chronicle* (yearbook) crew created a gift that was still giving fifty years later when their class celebrated its golden anniversary reunion.

team posted a 23–1 season, bringing the school its first prep round-ball championship since 1929. The 1955–56 swimming team members were also city champs. Track and baseball came too late in the spring to be included in the yearbook. We held our Rose Dance in the LaSalle Gym and the more formal Senior Prom at the elegant Rainbow Terrace Room.

High school reunions, usually somewhat surrealistic, prove that in some senses we can and do "go home again." The experience is a strange mixture of revisiting our adolescent insecurities and glorying in our classmates' levels of achievements, yet hoping to go them one better in some fashion or other. Some events, places and people seem almost unrecognizable, and others have altered amazingly little in a half century. In our reminiscences, some events seem as familiar as today's breakfast and others seem so exotic as to have happened to someone else.

Back then, of course, we were technically the High School Department of Christian Brothers College (CBC); except the college part had been dormant over most of the previous forty years. Thus, we high school boys *were* CBC. The Parkway Campus was ours, and the Walnut Grove Campus was nine years into the future. Like the "old boys" from the Adams Avenue campus had treated us in our day, we often act as if the Walnut Grove CBHS might not be quite the genuine article. But it is.

To learn more, see *The Christian Brothers in Memphis* by W.J. Battersby, PhD; the CBHS website at www.cbhs.org; or call CBU's Archives at (901)

321-3243. Also, check with the Memphis Room of our public library. It maintains a clipping file, accepts gifts of yearbooks and makes both available to researchers. It has strong yearbook runs for CBHS, MUS, Central, et cetera. Call (901) 415-2742 for more information.

Old School Ties

Advancing in Grace and Wisdom

In recent months and years, local media have placed great emphasis on the problems and the progress of city and county schools. This may be especially true because of the emotionally charged issues of the consolidation of school systems and the No Child Left Behind initiative.

In contrast, however, the ongoing excellence and vitality of several of our area's privately funded or independent schools is often overlooked. When failing to produce, independent schools rarely get repeated chances to redeem themselves. Many very fine old schools, such as the Higbee School, the Clara Conway Institute, the Memphis Military Academy and Pentecost-Garrison, currently exist only in a few memories, old newspaper files and Paul Coppock's books.

Other independent schools, however, have endured or returned. Despite the ravages of war, occupation, pestilence, economic depressions and competition with government-funded schools, five of this area's most venerable independent schools have celebrated centennial or even sesquicentennial anniversaries. These include: Saint Mary's Episcopal School (1847), St. Agnes Academy (1851), Christian Brothers High School (1871), Memphis University School (1893) and Hutchison School (1903). Most of these were founded prior to Tennessee creating "free," universal and mandatory government-operated schools. The five schools cited all have dramatic stories of their origins and struggles, their successes and failures and their tragedies and triumphs. Each has also published at least one book-length history, usually including the achievements and contributions of alumni. Each history also corrects misperceptions or explains some complexities regarding its institution's past. Treatments depicting their stories include:

Mary M. Davis, *A Remarkable Journey (The Story of St. Mary's Episcopal School, 1847–1997)*, 1998.

W.J. Battersby (Brother Clair), *The Christian Brothers in Memphis: A Chronicle of One Hundred Years, 1871–1971*, 1971.

John E. Harkins, *MUS Century Book*, 1993, 2003.
Leonard and Sara Frey, *Reflections on Learning and Life at Hutchison School*, 2003.
(St. Agnes published a book-length history in 1926. It is currently considering revising and updating its saga.)

The space available here is insufficient to include even a tiny historical narrative sketch of each school's history. We can, however, make some generalizations about them collectively. Most were founded as either religious schools or as proprietary ventures with denominational overtones. Each started in either downtown or midtown but has since relocated farther east. Each has a sanctioned historical marker, at the site of either its present campus or at a previous locale. (Hutchison School recently received and will soon dedicate its West Tennessee Historical Society–sanctioned marker.) Moreover, these schools' alumni have made social, civic, philanthropic, professional, economic and artistic contributions to the Memphis area vastly disproportionate to their numbers. Several of these schools have incubated other vital institutions for our city. St Agnes, for example, generated St. Peter's Orphanage, the Memphis Conservatory of Music (later Siena College) and St. Dominic School. The relationship between CBHS and CBU is much too complex to unravel here.

The Dominicans founded St. Agnes Academy in 1851, giving it a claim to being the oldest private school in Memphis. Its graduating class of 1912 looks both lively and lovely. *Courtesy of Special Collections, University of Memphis.*

Local Schools and Some of Their Products

Several generations of the Snowden family participated in the groundbreaking at 6191 Park Avenue for the 1955 rebirth of the city's legendary Memphis University School. *Courtesy Memphis University School Archives.*

Perhaps surprisingly, there has been a good bit of "cross pollination" among independent schools and also between independent and publicly funded schools. Many teachers and administrators have worked in both spheres. Perhaps the most conspicuous is Eugene Magevney. This early proprietary schoolmaster and activist Catholic layman was probably the Memphian most responsible for city government starting to underwrite the cost of public schooling. Given their common missions and interwoven histories, there should probably be more mutual cooperation and appreciation among independent and "public" schools.

Autumn 1955

A Renaissance for MUS

The original Memphis University School (MUS) opened in September 1893 and shut down forty-three years later, a casualty of the Great Depression and of greatly improved Memphis city schools. With the return of prosperity in the aftermath of World War II, a group of dedicated people and a cluster of unlikely circumstances coalesced to create a renaissance for MUS. Thus, MUS has two founding anniversaries, 1893 and 1955. The later school also had the legacies of three earlier institutions contributing to its rebirth.

The crisis that galvanized founders of Presbyterian Day School (PDS) and the new MUS to action was Miss Althea Pentecost's 1951 decision to liquidate Pentecost-Garrison School (PGS). Her cousin and junior partner, Miss Bea Garrison, had recently died, and Miss Pentecost's health also seemed in decline. Over thirty-six years, she had built a highly respected, kindergarten-through-ninth-grade boys' school of about 250 pupils. When she began to get offers to purchase her seven-acre site at Union and Hollywood, she first offered to sell the school and facilities to PGS parents and patrons. Although she did want to keep her educational legacy alive, she ultimately accepted the highest offer for her property. PGS did not reopen in the fall of 1951.

Coincidental to Miss Pentecost's decision, Second Presbyterian Church had recently moved to Poplar and Goodlett and had just opened a fledgling day school. When Dr. Tony Dick learned of the Pentecost-Garrison shutdown, he saw it as an opportunity. His church quickly revised its plans and expanded PDS to include grades kindergarten through nine. PDS initially absorbed about half of the faculty and students of PGS. It also hired Colonel Ross M. Lynn to head PDS and, ultimately, the new MUS. The patrons who created PDS had also committed to providing a comparable high school as soon as they reasonably could.

By 1953, an exploratory committee chaired by Alex Wellford had begun planning, assessing available resources and drafting a charter for a separate institution at another location. For both practical and sentimental reasons, this group decided to name its new corporation Memphis University School and to pattern it after its namesake. The group purchased a ninety-five-acre tract at Park and Ridgeway and hired an architect to design its buildings. Alumni of the defunct MUS, parents of PDS pupils and other patrons who wanted to make such a school a reality contributed generously in cash and kind. Board Chairman Wellford often remarked that God must have wanted their efforts to succeed because so many surprisingly favorable solutions had materialized whenever killer problems arose. Even so, the new school's physical plant had to be developed in stages.

The MUS founders broke ground for the school's initial structures (a hall of six classrooms, a cafeteria, two science labs and locker rooms) on March 28, 1955. Construction must have gone forward at a hectic pace because the school opened for classes in September. However, it waited until October 30 to hold its dedication. On that auspicious occasion, local dignitaries—including Mayor Walter Chandler, Southwestern College president Peyton Rhodes and Memphis State president J. Millard Smith—lent *gravitas* to the exercises. Howard G. Ford, principal and proprietor of the original MUS, passed the metaphorical torch to the new school, and the school's architect and building committee chairman ceremonially passed the new buildings' keys to Colonel Lynn.

Thus, the new MUS began in Spartan quarters, with only 95 students and seven overworked teachers. Since then, it has developed an elegant campus and enrolls about 630 students. MUS, however, retains the ideals and academic rigor emphasized at its rebirth. These are patterned on those of the its institutional ancestors, the first MUS, PGS and PDS.

Happy golden anniversary, renascent MUS!

The MUS Century Book, a book-length history of both incarnations of Memphis University School, is available in several local bookstores and through the MUS Office for Advancement. For more information about MUS, go online to www.musowls.org.

Crump machine stalwart Walter Chandler was Memphis's mayor, a local U.S. congressman, a *Baker v. Carr* Supreme Court case victor and father of (John) Wyeth Chandler (later councilman, mayor and judge). *Courtesy of Special Collections, University of Memphis.*

The Griders

An MUS Family's Tales of Two Wars

Among the many joys of being the institutional historian for Memphis University School is the fact that so many members of our community have dramatic stories to tell and that a good percentage of these can be recovered from a variety of sources. Among my favorites is that of (John) MacGavock Grider and his two sons, John M. Jr. and George W. All three of these lads attended the original MUS, and each of them served as a combat officer during a world war. Two of these young officers told their wartime stories in memoirs of sorts.

"Mac" Grider was killed when his plane was downed behind German lines in France in June 1918. Grider's close friend and fellow aviator Elliott White Springs revised and amplified Mac's wartime diary and published it serially in *Liberty* magazine in 1926. Entitled "War Birds, the Diary of an Unknown Aviator," this story has been republished in book form three times. Initially a popular success, it has received a good bit of enduring critical acclaim as well. Springs later gave $12,500 in royalties (a fairly princely sum at that time) from *War Birds* to the Grider family for Mac's sons.

After completing their college preparatory educations at MUS, both of Mac Grider's boys attended the U.S. Naval Academy and served as officers during World War II. As a submarine commander in the Pacific Theater, George's boat sank record-setting numbers of enemy ships during the war. He relates his adventures as a sub commander in his memoir, *War Fish*, which he wrote with his longtime friend and *Commercial Appeal* columnist Lydel Sims.

George's older brother, John, made a career of the navy following the war and retired at the rank of captain. In his later years, John devoted himself to public betterment causes in Memphis. After his death in 1984, Grace-St. Luke's School established a scholarship in his honor.

George might also have continued his military career, but health issues forced him out of the navy in 1947. After graduating from the University of Virginia's law school, he returned to Memphis and practiced law. A devoted community activist and reform Democrat, George soon entered politics at the local level. He managed Mayor Edmund Orgill's 1955 election campaign and then himself won election to the (now supplanted) Shelby County Quarterly Court in 1960. George capped his political career by defeating thirteen-term, Crump-machine-holdover congressman Clifford Davis in the

Local Schools and Some of Their Products

George W. Grider (right) and his friend and "as told to" collaborator Lydel Sims signed books when *War Fish* was published in 1958. *Courtesy of Special Collections, University of Memphis.*

1964 Democratic primary election. George then won the general election but served for only two years before losing to Republican Dan Kuykendall.

There is so much more to the Griders' stories, but there is not sufficient space to elaborate on them in this column.

War Birds *Revisited and Revised*

Most of my story focusing on MacGavock Grider and the book *War Birds* was based on information that I had been familiar with since 1993. Recently, however, George W. Grider Jr. informed me that there is a 2003 video documentary based on the *War Birds* story. This fifty-seven-minute DVD, directed by Robert Clem, tells a very powerful story, but one significantly different from traditional accounts in and about the book.

The video story begins as the book does, with MacGavock Grider leaving home to become an Allied pilot during World War I. He quickly became close friends with fellow volunteers Larry Callahan and Elliott White Springs. All three were "born hell-raisers." Entering flight training in December 1917, their days were devoted primarily to eating, drinking, fighting, womanizing, braggadocio, adolescent pranks and the thrill of flying. Springs was the leader of the three, but Grider was more popular. The three were assigned to the command of Colonel Billy Bishop, who, like these "Three Musketeers," was considered a maverick and imposed little discipline on his flyers.

The mortality rate for pilots in World War I was horrendous. In 1917, the average Allied pilot survived only about three weeks at the front. Antiaircraft fire and superior German planes placed Allied pilots at a disadvantage. Our three lads arrived at the front in May 1918, conscious of the risks but not initially engulfed by the gnawing fear that would soon become oppressive. As they saw members of their cohort killed in action, they soon viewed their own deaths as coming in just a matter of time and were determined to "die well" when that time came. Oddly, the all-absorbing fear affected them most between flights. When aloft, they felt intensely alive, searching for enemy targets. As they became seasoned by combat, none of the three expected to survive the war. Before the war ended, the twenty-four-year-old Springs was said to have looked forty and felt ninety.

On June 18, 1918, Grider and Springs were aloft on patrol about sixteen miles behind enemy lines. They had headed back toward base when Grider peeled off to chase a German plane. Separated in the clouds, Springs returned to base, and Grider was shot down and killed. Springs seems to have felt an irrational guilt about Grider's death.

Both Callahan and Springs survived the war but had been traumatized. Later, Springs published their raw story, first as a magazine serial and later as a book. Thought to be the "most accurate and wrenching" story of fighter pilots to emerge from the war, it inspired dozens of movies, including *Wings*, the 1927–28 Academy Award–winning best picture. T.E. Lawrence termed the book "immortal"; William A. Percy said that it possessed all "the ardor, idiocy, and heartbreak of youth."

Robert Clem's DVD claims that *War Birds* is really the story of Elliott White Springs rather than that of Mac Grider. Accordingly, Clem makes Springs the real protagonist of his documentary and includes the latter's troubled life following the war. Perhaps additional research will provide sufficient evidence to assess the accuracy of Clem's revisions. Perhaps not.

Richard Halliburton Revisited

I love to read and write about travel and adventure, Memphis and Memphians, topics related to Memphis University School (MUS) and various persons who share my addiction to writing. Richard Halliburton encapsulates all of these elements, and he keeps being rediscovered, sometimes reinvented. Former Memphian Carolyn Treanor, CEO of Sunflower Circle Productions, has recently undertaken an ambitious, multifaceted project to restore Halliburton to his proper place in our nation's pantheon.

Halliburton grew up in Memphis, attending Hutchison and MUS before finishing at Lawrenceville and Princeton. While in college, he signed on as an ordinary seaman on a Europe-bound freighter and then "bummed around" Britain and France. He wrote home frequently, relating his excitement at the places he visited and the historical personages and events he encountered. His father, Wesley, showed his letters to *Commercial Appeal* editor C.P.J. Mooney, who began publishing and syndicating them in 1922. Richard was soon on his way to becoming the best-known travel/adventure writer and lecturer of his era and the best-known Memphian in the world.

Halliburton's adventures and accomplishments are the stuff of legends, sometimes myths. Even discounting for embellishment, his encounters in dangerous and remote places still make for compelling reading. Exciting place names like Timbuktu, the Taj Mahal, Popocatepetl and Chichen-Itza are sprinkled throughout his biography like rare, exotic spices. He climbed Mount Olympus, the Matterhorn and Mount Fujiyama. He swam

In the 1920s and '30s, handsome Memphian Richard Halliburton was the most popular travel and adventure writer in the world. Many of his books are still in print in 2009. *Courtesy of Memphis University School Archives.*

the Hellespont, the Panama Canal and the Sea of Galilee. He sampled the lives of Borneo headhunters, French foreign legionnaires and Devil's Island convicts.

Halliburton and a companion completed an around-the-world aviation tour in a two-seater biplane that he called the *Flying Carpet.* They had thrills and chills aplenty. Halliburton nearly fell out of the plane during a barrel roll in Nepal; he nearly stalled the plane when he stood up in the airstream to snap a picture of Mount Everest's summit; and he nearly killed them both when he snagged an anchor line in the *Flying Carpet's* propeller. Their "survivor" escapades were genuine, unlike today's phony "reality shows."

Chronically short of money, Halliburton sometimes took "shortcuts" or "used people" to achieve his purposes. Very early, Richard had expressed his disdain for the mundane in life. Addressing the placid and commonplace, he wrote to his father that he intended "to avoid that condition…and [make his life] as vivid as possible." He continued that when his time came to die, "I'll be especially happy if I am spared a stupid, common death in bed."

Richard Halliburton died at the midpoint of his last great adventure. His crew of twelve was sailing a custom-made Chinese junk, the *Sea Dragon,* across the Pacific when it foundered in heavy seas. His final dispatch from the ship, March 24, 1939, expressed the clever bravado that had characterized much of his adult life.

Google accesses 177,000 items on Richard Halliburton and the availability of eight of his books. Thus, Treanor has a great deal to work with and a potentially fertile market for her videographers' recapitulation of our "MUS old boy's" most excellent adventures.

Miss Charl Ormand Williams

Shelby County's Educator Extraordinaire

Probably no individual, except possibly her sister Mabel, did more in the early twentieth century to advance education in Shelby County schools than Charl O. Williams (1885–1969). Born and reared in tiny Arlington, Tennessee, Charl was the third of Crittenden and Minnie Williams's six children. She attended local schools, graduating from Arlington High School in 1903. Later that year, she taught at Millington; the following two years, she served as principal at Bartlett's secondary school. From 1906 to 1912, she taught at Germantown High School, serving as its principal the last three years. She then worked for two years at the newly opened West

Local Schools and Some of Their Products

Former Shelby County suffragette, teacher, principal and school superintendent Charl Williams became field secretary for the National Education Association and a nationally prominent Democratic Party leader. *Courtesy of Special Collections, University of Memphis.*

Tennessee State Normal School (now the University of Memphis), before succeeding her sister Mabel as superintendent of Shelby County Schools.

Although she was only twenty-nine when she became superintendent in 1914, between taking office and 1922, Miss Charl revolutionized Shelby County's school system. She revised the curriculum, introduced physical activities, doubled student attendance, significantly increased the system's funding and added a number of new buildings. The system rose to national prominence; by one account, it was ranked sixth among America's rural school systems.

As the school system rose to national prominence, so did Charl. After holding a number of subordinate offices in educational associations, in 1921 the National Education Association (NEA) elected her to its presidency. Upon taking office, she was the youngest, the first rural and the first southern female educator to be so honored. The success of her tenure as president immediately led the NEA to offer her a salaried executive position as the organization's national field secretary. She accepted the NEA's offer and continued in that capacity until she retired in 1950. She served with distinction, traveling thirty to fifty thousand miles per year, lecturing widely, serving on various boards and committees and writing numerous articles. She also wrote two books on educational reform: *Our Public Schools*

(1934) and *Schools for Democracy* (1939). Moreover, she was often interviewed or otherwise the subject of dozens of magazine and newspaper articles. Long a contributor to civic betterment and female advancement, Williams capped her service in these areas as president of the National Federation of Business and Professional Women's Clubs from 1935 to 1937. She was the first educator to ever serve in that post. As a national figure, her biographical sketch appeared in *Who's Who in America* for many years.

Charl Williams could not have operated effectively within national educational and professional circles without having shrewd political instincts. She would never have risen as rapidly as she did within the Shelby County School System if her family had not had cordial relations with the Crump machine. Moreover, she worked closely with Shelby County's delegation in getting Tennessee's legislature to ratify the Nineteenth (woman's suffrage) Amendment. She became the first Tennessee woman to serve on the Democratic National Committee; she served as a delegate to her party's 1920 national convention; and she became the first woman of either major party to serve as national vice chairman. She stayed active in Democratic politics and maintained a friendship with Eleanor Roosevelt into their later years.

Given her obvious political acuity, the terms of her departure from Shelby County are shrouded in a bit of mystery. As the time for her contract renewal approached in 1922, rumors abounded that the county machine intended to oust her. In anticipation of such action, Charl accepted the job offer from the NEA and tendered her resignation to the county court. Despite the Crump machine's influence, the county squires begged her to stay on as superintendent. They even offered to match the $7,500 field secretary's salary and find her additional resources for upgrading the county's school system. For whatever reasons, Charl declined. Then, our indefatigable Shelby County "school marm" departed to make her considerable impact on school systems across our nation.

As an off-again, on-again (some would say renegade) archivist, I am always delighted to learn that some documentary gem that might easily have been forever lost has found its way into an appropriate repository for preservation and for access by researchers. Such was the case with a 1922 "Memory Book" presented to Miss Charl O. Williams when she departed as superintendent of the Shelby County School system that year. Her teachers and her colleagues then serving in county government, headquartered in the Shelby County Courthouse, presented her with a book of photographic prints. The subjects were themselves and the new schoolhouses that Miss Williams had lobbied so successfully to bring to fruition.

Miss Williams presumably had possession of the book for many decades. Upon her demise, her nephew apparently had it until his death in recent years. Thereupon, a grand niece loaned it to another party to have it copied for the County Board of Education. There is conflicting evidence regarding the chain of custody thereafter, but the book wound up in the Shelby County Archives, where Miss Williams's great niece wants it to remain.

Professor Jester and Central High School's Rise to Eminence

How ironic that a man as purposeful, productive and influential as Professor Charles P. Jester should have had a surname that might suggest frivolous or even clownish behavior. As Central High School's principal, he was the chief catalyst for and symbol of its stellar performance and reputation. Thus, this Jester must be taken seriously.

Born in 1872 of hardy pioneer stock and reared while working hard on a farm near Jackson, Tennessee, young Charles finished secondary school by age sixteen. Quickly obtaining his certification, he began teaching in rural summer schools as he worked his way through college. From 1896 until 1908, he served as principal and teacher in a series of West Tennessee's rural schools. In 1908, he moved to Memphis and served successively as principal of Gordon, Maury and Bruce Schools before being named to lead Central High in 1918.

At Central, Jester became an icon. He quickly revised the school's curriculum and pushed through accreditation from the Southern Association of Colleges and Schools. He then set about gathering and directing a superb faculty and staff, which ultimately made Central one of the South's most highly regarded prep schools. It became, in essence, a "magnet" school, setting standards for the Mid-South's other public schools. Jester's team set up a strong ROTC program, pioneered working with student government, established a significant college scholarship fund, quadrupled the library's holdings, brought stereopticons and motion pictures into the classrooms and, according to an obit on file at the Memphis and Shelby County Rome of Memphis Public Library, "effected similar improvements in all departments and activities."

At retirement, Jester estimated that more than ten thousand students had graduated from Central during his tenure there. Over a twenty-eight-year span, the six-foot, three-inch, two-hundred-pound Jester stayed in excellent physical condition. Even late in his career, he could handle any of the boys if they "tried to get out of line." Although most students viewed him as stern, they also thought of him as fair. When a large percentage of the school's ROTC boys blatantly disobeyed direct instructions, however, they learned just how tough he could be.

Jester gave the offenders their choice between suspension with a parental conference or receiving a paddling. On the premise that he couldn't or wouldn't whip them all, about seventy of the boys opted for the latter. Although the boys' decision surprised Mr. Jester, he knew that he couldn't back down. He got the wood shop to furnish five good paddles, and with male teachers funneling the boys through a small room, Jester had each one lean over a bench to receive his licks. Such strenuous activity gave the boys bruised behinds, and it thoroughly exhausted the good professor. He expressed confidence that the lads bore him no ill will in this matter; he believed that those he had whipped that day would have fought on his behalf had an occasion presented itself.

Jester followed the careers of former students with great interest and affection, encouraging and helping many of them to realize their full potential.

"Professor" Charles P. Jester was both the catalyst for and the main symbol of Central High School's conspicuous excellence during the early twentieth century. *Courtesy of Charles P. Jester III.*

Local Schools and Some of Their Products

He often expressed his pride in their successes and their demonstrations of personal integrity. Challenged on this score with the example of George Kelly Barnes, Jester retorted that "in his [chosen] field of endeavor, he was [also] outstanding." Barnes, better known as "Machine Gun Kelly," had made the FBI's ten most wanted list.

Jester's religious, civic and family aspects of life were all quite satisfying and supportive of his career. Upon his forced retirement from Central in 1946, Jester served as dean of the Memphis College of Accountancy until 1960, when prolonged illness forced his final retirement. Thus, he spent a total of seventy years as teacher and principal. While at Central, he boasted that he had only missed one day of school (attending an aunt's funeral in another town) and had *never* been tardy. Over his long career, Professor Jester had demanded excellence of himself and of those around him. Rarely was he ever disappointed.

St. Anne School and the Class of 1952

No doubt, Thomas Wolf was on to something when he famously said that we "can't go home again." However, with a proper stimulus to prod our memories, we can sometimes make spectacular imaginative leaps back in time. The accompanying photograph provides a case in point. It captures St. Anne School's graduating class of 1952. Recovering a digitized version of this shot and conferring with a half dozen classmates, we have collectively identified all but one of our fellow graduates. We would love to know the name of the tall girl on the extreme left of the second row. Many of us were fairly new to the school in '52 and memory dims a bit over nearly six decades.

St. Anne's parish and school had grown out of a mission church called St. Sebastian, operating from temporary quarters prior to World War I. It mainly served Buntyn-area Italian truck farmers, who especially venerated the "twice-martyred" Milanese saint. However, Father Thomas Nenon was of Irish extraction and was particularly devoted to St. Anne, mother of the Virgin Mary. Appointed pastor in 1937, Father Tom lobbied successfully to change the parish's patron saint.

Nenon's appointment also corresponded with his congregation's move to permanent quarters on Highland at Spottswood Avenue. The new property provided ample room for a parish school. Staffed by Sisters of Charity of Nazareth, Kentucky, with an enrollment of one hundred children, the school initially occupied a one-story, three-room wooden building. The school's

From left to right, top row: Glenn Cowles, George Stokes, David Bauxbaum, Billie Ellard, Ed Shea, Carl Laux, Eddie Schrimsher, Wayne Hoffman, Ray Kallaher Jr., Neff Webber, Marion Brown and John Harkins. *Second row:* John Stokes, Floyd Angleton, Ada Darnell, Pat Patterson, Mary Dot Rea, Edith Ann Arnold, Carole Schaffler, Barbara Baker, Kitty Vaughn, Paula Pongetti and Bernard Tragarz. *Front row:* Judith Creigh, Jane Schnieder, Rosemarie Stevens, Rose Anne Anneritone, Mary Jo Laughter, Mary Agnes Wade, Pat Wade, Marcia Kay Sperry, Helen McDonald, Mary Anne Cardosi, Elizabeth Anne Bell, June Marie Powers and Ernie Youngblood. (Spellings of names above are often phonetic; please forgive any errors.)

quarters remained stunted through the scarcities of the Depression and World War II. By 1948–49, however, St. Anne constructed a much larger, three-story brick school building, with its basement and future cafeteria used for religious services. The new facility enabled a major extension of parish boundaries and allowed the school to dramatically increase its enrollment.

The thirty-seven students shown in the accompanying photograph composed what was likely St. Anne's largest graduating class to that time. However, there were other pupils in that class between 1948 and 1952. Among those missing from the photo include Jackie Landry (stricken with polio), Mary Elizabeth Staelens and Estelle Eggleston (later of Hollywood fame as Stella Stevens), whose families had moved away, and a large, quiet, redhaired boy named Anderson. During those three years at the "new" St. Anne's, our class's teachers were Sister Alice Richard, Sister Ellen Meriam and Sister Mary Ophelia (principal), for grades six, seven and eight, respectively. We have forwarded a copy of the graduation shot to St. Anne School for its digital archival holdings.

Local Schools and Some of Their Products

Going over thirteen- and fourteen-year-old faces in this picture and comparing notes with some classmates has evoked a flood tide of memories. Perhaps our reawakened memories and emotions are sufficiently strong for us to carry out a class of '52 reunion in the not-too-distant future. Certainly, St. Anne School would welcome additions to its archival holdings. To lend or contribute images or documents, please contact Ms. Cristy Perry at cperry@stannehighland.net or see the website at www.stannehighland.net/school.htm.

Children's Histories of Memphis

Opening a New Book

Among my favorite and most frequently bandied opinions, I rank the following four pretty high: 1. Most Memphians don't know nearly enough about their community's history to function as good citizens. 2. Even primary school students should start learning meaningful history early in life. 3. Local history is very enjoyable and physically close enough to be most meaningful. 4. Knowing local history provides a super foundation for mastering history's broader vistas. But where does one send young people to begin their search for their place in the world? Thanks to popular local historian Perre Magness, there is now a solid response to that pesky question. Drawing on her extensive background in Mid-South history, Magness has just published her tenth book, *Memphis: A Children's History*.

Magness's latest book is probably the third children's history of Memphis to be published and is arguably the best of the three. The earliest such work is *Tales of a River Town: A Child's History of Memphis*, written by Patricia Morrison Leeker and Mimsey Wood Frazier and published by Friends of the Pink Palace Museum in 1969. Second in time is *City on the Bluff: History and Heritage of Memphis*, authored by Rebecca L. Robertson and published by the Friends of Memphis and Shelby County Libraries in 1987. Both earlier works are helpful, but both have also been out of print for many years and are difficult to locate even in local libraries. Consequently, Magness's new book is doubly welcome. It is now readily available in several local bookstores, and it appeared in time for holiday giving. Unfortunately, it appeared too late for me to feature it in our December issue of the *Best Times*.

For sixteen years, local historian Perre Magness wrote her popular "Past Times" column for the *Commercial Appeal*. Most recent of her eight books is her children's history of Memphis. *Courtesy of Perre Magness.*

Memphis: A Children's History is unique in several respects. Magness had several children (whom she refers to as her "editors") read and react to her work as she was writing. Its illustrations, by Michelle Duckworth, are often patterned after familiar historical images but also display a stylistic consistency. Most are rendered in full color and have a primitive quality that suits the book and appeals to both children and adults. Perhaps the use of so much color and the number and size of images contribute to the book's cost of $19.95—not cheap for a forty-two-page paperback book. However, those adults whom I have observed eagerly examining this book seemed undismayed by its price.

It is not possible to provide a very comprehensive retelling of our city's history in such a brief, amply illustrated work. Even so, Magness employs a significant emphasis on social history, including music, religion and the roles of women and ethnic minorities. She has indicated that her very young "editors" especially liked learning about the bloody stuff, like the *Sultana* (riverboat) disaster and the city's deadly yellow fever plagues.

Perhaps Magness should have had adult historians vet her book as well. Some are likely to cite matters of fact and tone with which they disagree, but there is certainly nothing new in that. Magness, who recently established a local history lecture series at Hutchison School, is a master storyteller and recounts some of our city's best stories in this book. Doubtless, this latest children's history will help a new generation of Memphians become more self-aware and, it is to be hoped, better stewards of our city's rich heritage.

PART IV

Places to Find Portions of Our Shared Past

"Cousin Ellen's" Historical Legacies

The Origins of the Davies Manor Plantation Museum Home

Ellen Davies Rodgers (1903–1994) was a true "steel magnolia," comparable in many respects to a force of nature. She was a smart, tough woman, with a physical presence that matched her imperious will and her enormous social and political clout. Like her political patron E.H. Crump, Mrs. Rodgers and her antics inspired at least one good story from anyone even casually associated with her. Listening to "Miss Ellen" tales, she emerges as a stereotype, sometimes a caricature, of a persona from the pen of William Faulkner, Tennessee Williams or even Florence King. Vignettes about "Cousin Ellen" are usually tied to at least one of her major legacies for our area's history.

Ellen served as our official Shelby County historian for about thirty years, operating very much on her own terms. She penned and published ten books, mainly on Episcopal Church history and Shelby County's pioneer past. For many decades, she was a mover and shaker in the Daughters of the American Revolution, with a local chapter named for one of her ancestors. She also developed much of her twenty-five-hundred-acre plantation into the posh communities of Stonebridge and Davieshire. In so doing, she immortalized select friends and relatives by naming streets in those subdivisions after them.

Probably eclipsing her roles as organizer, philanthropist and chronicler would have been Mrs. Rodgers's impact as a player in local educational and political affairs. She made a significant impact in educational circles, serving as teacher and department head at Memphis State College, briefly

Above: Wilson's General Merchandise Store at Arlington (northeast Shelby County) remains open but is now more of a community museum than a competitor of today's "big box" department stores. *Courtesy of Special Collections, University of Memphis.*

Left: Ellen Davies Rodgers and her husband, Hillman, often hosted historical, civic, social and political events at her ancestral home, Davies Manor. She also served for thirty years as county historian. *Courtesy of Special Collections, University of Memphis.*

as principal at Lausanne School for Girls and Arlington High School and on the Shelby County Board of Education.

Although rooted in her staunch support for the Crump regime, Mrs. Rodgers's political clout survived Mr. Crump's demise by four decades. Wielding her influence in the 1960s and '70s, she demanded, and got, a bridge built across Interstate Highway 40 to keep her northern and southern landholdings connected. She was also the driving force in amending Tennessee's constitution to require the approval of a majority of county voters outside the city in order to consolidate Memphis and Shelby County governments. When Al Gore was first seeking the nation's presidency, she summoned him to attend one of her social functions and to personally pick up her campaign contribution. Gore duly shifted his itinerary, attended her gathering and hobnobbed, but he allegedly departed with a distressingly small check.

Perhaps the most conspicuous and enduring of all of Mrs. Rodgers's legacies will be the preservation of her family's antebellum "plantation" home and outbuildings. In the 1930s, Ellen was farsighted enough to preserve the hand-hewn, two-story log house known as Davies Manor. She made it a gathering place for local and state heritage groups and turned it into a museum home. Later, she had it placed on the National Register of Historic Places and opened it to the public. Finally, she created and endowed the nonprofit Davies Manor Association (DMA) to perpetuate the manor's restoration, preservation and operations. Thank you, Ellen!

Because of the indefatigable efforts of Jeanne Crawford, Marilyn Van Eynde and Randall Langston, plus the diligent work by the DMA's docents and board of trustees, the Davies Manor complex is becoming an increasingly authentic and accessible gem for interpreting the Mid-South's rural frontier history and culture. It hosts a number of unique historical gatherings each

Davies Manor's museum house dates from at least the early 1830s and furnishes splendid examples of how Shelby County's frontier farm families lived in the mid-nineteenth century. *Courtesy of Davies Manor Association.*

The Gotten family donated this dogtrot log cabin to Liberty Land theme park in the 1970s. When Liberty Land closed in 2006, this cabin was dismantled and moved to Davies Manor Plantation. *Courtesy of Davies Manor Association.*

year and is available for group historical activities, as well as for weddings and other private assemblages.

Davies Manor is open for tours and is located at 9336 Davies Plantation Road, just north of I-40 and one mile or so west of the Lakeland–Canada Road exit. For more information, access www.daviesmanorplantation.org, call the DMA staff at (901) 386-0715 or e-mail daviesmn@bellsouth.net.

More on Our Area's Frontier Farmstead Heritage

In 2006, a half dozen members of the Davies Manor Association (DMA) rallied at Liberty Land to assess the feasibility of preserving several historic log structures that were at risk of demolition under emerging plans for revamping the fairgrounds. The DMA Board was considering moving one or more of these buildings to Davies Manor. Its purpose was not just to preserve the cabins but also to recreate the authentic atmosphere of a nineteenth-century Shelby County farmstead.

Places to Find Portions of Our Shared Past

News stories about closing Liberty Land prompted Dr. Nick Gotten to inquire about the fate slated for the dogtrot log cabin that his parents had donated in 1975. The response was that, if the cabin could be preserved by the DMA, the fair would make it available. During our visit to Liberty Land, we learned that there were actually five nineteenth-century log structures that might be available. With such an opportunity in the offing, DMA members needed to learn a lot about moving log houses as quickly as possible.

At the suggestion of local photographer and historian Robert Dye, a DMA committee quickly booked a visit to Ames Plantation. Ames has created a mid-nineteenth-century farmstead near Grand Junction, Tennessee (about sixty miles due east of Memphis). We toured the Ames Heritage Village and enjoyed a long and very fruitful conversation with Assistant Director Jamie Evans. Mr. Evans revealed both why and how Ames personnel are creating and maintaining their nineteenth-century farmstead. Even those of us steeped in West Tennessee lore had little knowledge of the plantation's frontier atmosphere and its educational mission.

The Heritage Village's log structures have been culled from various other sites on the extensive Ames Plantation. This farmstead now contains a dogtrot cabin, a smokehouse, a corncrib, a barn, two slave cabins and a blacksmith's forge. In addition, there is a one-room schoolhouse and the "Stencil House" (which is undergoing restoration). The setting is a typical nineteenth-century, West Tennessee farm layout. Accordingly, it provides the ideal venue for an annual Ames Heritage Festival. In this one-day gathering, about 125 craftspersons, reenactors, musicians, et cetera, give on-site demonstrations of what West Tennessee farm life was like circa 1850. They provide ongoing, authentic re-creations of folk arts, frontier work routines and our nineteenth-century musical heritage. About four thousand visitors enjoyed this festival in October 2005.

Mr. Evans also gave the DMA group basic information on the problems, costs and labor involved in creating the Ames Heritage Village. He included possible sources for consultant services and for helping to fund such a project. He also taught us that we had a lot more to learn before going forward with moving the Gotten cabin from midtown Memphis to the Davies Manor in east Bartlett. The examples of the Ames farmstead and festival, however, made creating something similar in Shelby County seem like an even worthier goal.

The Davies Manor Association has moved the Gotten cabin and another medium-sized log house from the fairgrounds to its property in east Bartlett. Restoration of both structures is nearly completed, and they will be integrated into the sort of educational facility that Mrs. Rodgers envisioned when she created what is becoming a frontier farmstead museum complex.

Kirby Farm House and Shelby County History

The site of the Kirby Farm House at 6792 Poplar Pike has been occupied since at least 1834. At that time, Colonel Eppy White, for whom the community of White's Station was later named, owned this land. Sitting on a natural ridge, the house has looked southward at a series of "highways" over the last 170 years. Initially, there was the old Cherokee Trace, probably taking advantage of existing buffalo trails. Upon European settlement in the area, the Alabama or State Line Road was "improved" along what had been the Indian trace. Later, a plank road was built to accommodate heavier traffic, and travelers paid tolls in order to use it. In 1848, tolls ranged from no charge for herding small groups of animals to twenty cents each for wagons drawn by five or more draft animals. By 1852, the Memphis and Charleston Railroad ran past the farmstead, offering a high-speed, inexpensive connection between Memphis and Germantown.

In 1838, Colonel White sold this "Pea Ridge" farm to a North Carolina transplant named Wilks Brooks. Following Brooks's death in 1849, his heirs sold the land, and it changed hands nine times between 1853 and 1869, a testimony to the speculative nature of landholding in Shelby County at that time. The house served as a refuge from yellow fever contagion during the 1870s and was given its Victorian ornamentation in the early 1890s. In 1898,

The Kirby Farm House contains elements dating from the 1830s but was later expanded and redecorated as shown above. Norfolk Southern Railroad later cut off its southerly access from Poplar Pike. *Courtesy of Walter D. Wills, III.*

Trolleys revolutionized urban transit and the city's demographic makeup. This particular trolley carried passengers on Poplar Avenue. *Courtesy of Special Collections, University of Memphis.*

John A. Kirby, a Virginia-born transplant and Confederate veteran, bought the property. Fittingly, Kirby married Ann Eliza Brooks, a granddaughter of the previous owner Wilks Brooks. Kirby had extensive holdings in the Mid-South, and the Kirby Farm House was the headquarters for his diverse eight-thousand-plus acres of farming operations. The house has been in this family ever since.

As the population moved east from Memphis and west from Germantown, most of the Kirby estate was developed to one use or another. The family, however, has kept and preserved the house and extensively restored it and its outbuildings. Walter D. Wills III, great-great-grandson of Wilks Brooks and great-grandson of John Kirby, has preserved this ten-acre tract and its rural characteristics. He has also worked hard to find an adaptive reuse of the property that will sustain its antiquities for the education and enjoyment of all mid-southerners. Over two decades, he has made it available to numerous historical societies, scouting groups, American history students and teachers and various civic and patriotic organizations. Whenever feasible, Walter personally conducts tours of the property, lovingly explaining every detail to appreciative visitors.

The Norfolk and Southern Railroad owns and still uses the right of way just south of Kirby Farm. During recent work on its tracks, the company interrupted use of the crossing between the house and Poplar Pike. Now, because of policies restricting the use of railroad crossings to private property, Kirby Farm is cut off from its Poplar Pike access. This can be likened to having its face removed. A back road from the much busier Poplar Avenue may prohibit restoring the farm's grade crossing and ruin the whole south-facing orientation and cultural integrity of the house, which is one of Shelby County's most significant cultural gems. What a cruel blow this will be to local history if Norfolk Southern refuses to remedy this unfortunate situation.

Seeking the Mid-South's Cotton Heritage

When longtime mid-southerners think of celebrating the role of cotton in our history, we usually turn our thoughts to "Cotton Carnival." Cotton was so central to the fabric of our regional economy that local business interests founded the carnival in 1931 to counter the effects of the Great Depression. Patterned deliberately after Memphis's earlier Mardi Gras observances, the carnival's purposes were to have a good time, raise morale and promote the use of cotton. According to A. Arthur Halle's "History of the Memphis Cotton Carnival" in the *West Tennessee Historical Society Papers* (1952), however, the carnival never focused strongly on cotton's historical impact on the Mid-South. Moreover, in recent decades Cotton Carnival morphed into the Great River Carnival, which shares the city's festival spotlight with Memphis in May.

Neither the Pink Palace nor the Mississippi River Museum emphasizes cotton's story in proportion to its impact on Mid-South history. There are, however, two exciting and complementary museum projects currently underway that will interpret the Mid-South's cotton heritage. Memphis cotton man Calvin Turley is heading a group that is installing a cotton museum in the Cotton Exchange Building at Front and Union. Under discussion for at least two decades, this highly desirable amenity had sufficient space and funding to become a reality before 2006.

More immediately available to those fascinated by cotton's history is the Cotton Museum of the South at "Green Frog Village," just north of Bells, Tennessee, on U.S. Highway 412. On March 5, 2005, the West Tennessee

Places to Find Portions of Our Shared Past

The Cotton Carnival, with its faux royalty, secret societies, street parades and elaborate balls, was for decades the city's "party with a purpose." *Courtesy of the Memphis and Shelby Room, Memphis Public Library.*

Historical Society and the Tennessee Historical Society renewed an old tradition and held a joint meeting at this small museum village. Dr. John Freeman and his wife, Nancy, conducted an hour-long tour for the two groups. The Freemans offered an unpretentious description of the "hands-on history" that they are preserving for future generations. Very much a work in progress, Green Frog Village at present has a log meeting building, a small country church, a one-room country schoolhouse, a blacksmith's forge, a commissary store, other farm outbuildings and a nearly restored, early twentieth-century, four-stand cotton gin house. An arboretum and an incipient wildflower path also add interest to the Freemans' labor of love. Our hosts and their village experience were truly delightful. For more information go to www.cottonmuseumofthesouth.tn.org or call the museum office at (731) 663-3319.

Of course, for those who primarily want information on the history of our area's cotton industry, there is a great deal available in print. Probably the best popular source for cotton's role in Memphis's economic history is Robert A. Sigafoos's *Cotton Row to Beale Street: A Business History of Memphis.* Bob's chapter on "The Power Brokers of Front Street" reveals the extent to

Cotton provided the basis for Mid-South prosperity for more than a century. Loose cotton entered the gin and later emerged from it seeded, compressed and bailed for shipment. *Courtesy of Special Collections, University of Memphis.*

which cotton remained the core of our local economy well into the twentieth century. (Cotton is still the Mid-South's number-one cash crop.) Sigafoos's detailed, yet highly readable, history is still in print twenty-five years after publication. It is usually available at local bookstores or can be ordered from the West Tennessee Historical Society.

Of more recent vintage and more scholarly content, yet still highly readable, is Lynette Boney Wrenn's brilliant analytical history of the creation, development and importance of cotton's byproducts industries. Her *Cinderella of the New South: A History of the Cottonseed Industry, 1855–1955* (University of Tennessee Press, 1995) seems likely to remain the definitive treatment of this long neglected subject.

As is usually the case, vignettes on cotton-related subjects are to be found in Paul R. Coppock's six volumes of Mid-South history, and longer articles on cotton history appear in the *West Tennessee Historical Society Papers.*

Where Cotton Still Reigns

Unable to tour the Memphis Cotton Museum right after it opened, I have had occasion to visit it three times in recent weeks. Attending an independent

Places to Find Portions of Our Shared Past

Front Street was known as "Cotton Row." Its cotton merchants crowded daily onto the trading floor of the Memphis Cotton Exchange, the economic heart of the nation's cotton markets. *Courtesy of Memphis Cotton Museum.*

schoolteacher's meeting, taking in a museum lecture on local world-class photographer J.C. Coovert's work and hosting January's West Tennessee Historical Society in the museum were extraordinarily meaningful and enjoyable learning experiences. The museum gives visitors a strong overview of the entire history of the world's foremost miracle fiber. Moreover, it is all shown from the former trading floor of the world's largest inland cotton trading center.

Between 1920 and 1978, the giant chalkboard of market quotes was the backbone of a national and international communications system for cotton trading. Then the advent of the computer and Internet allowed traders to have instant and universal access to the world's cotton market data. No longer needing proximity to the trading floor for tracking the market, Memphis traders gradually deserted "Cotton Row" for offices elsewhere. However, our city still reigns as the world center for "spot cotton" trading and for the world's largest cotton-trading firms. Without the cotton bales and samples strewn along Front Street, however, there is little downtown to remind us of cotton's role as a dynamic engine of the Mid-South's economy. Today's youth simply don't realize that our area's cotton trade is much more than a mere historical footnote.

Distressed by this situation, some of the remaining downtown traders set about preserving this chapter of our history in a very tangible way: they decided to turn the exchange's unused trading floor into a state-of-the-art theme museum. Local history buffs had been clamoring for such an amenity for decades. Even so, from inception to completion, the museum required nearly eight years of planning, fundraising, acquiring artifacts, working with professionals, designing and creating displays, producing audiovisual installations, setting up a nonprofit status and a good deal more. Small groups of volunteers from the local cotton community and a few professionals have created a small, but world-class, museum. Set and display designer Scott Blake, mural painter David Mah, award-winning videographer Willy Bearden, former Wonders architect Louis Pounders and other stars in their fields have crafted a venue that tells the full story of cotton and its impact on our history, economics, science and culture. That story is available daily to tourists from around the world and to schoolchildren from across our region. It is definitely an experience not to be missed.

The museum, located at 65 Union Avenue (at Front Street), is open Tuesday through Saturday from 10:00 a.m. to 5:00 p.m. and on Sunday from noon to 5:00 p.m. Arrangements for group tours with interpretative guides can be booked by phoning at least one week in advance. Finally, the museum welcomes docents to help tell its story. For information on setting up a tour, becoming a volunteer docent or anything else related to the Cotton Museum, call (901) 531-7826.

The Downtown Historical Parks "Issue"

Political figures have recently suggested that we should change the names of three of our historical downtown municipal parks. This proposal has sparked hot passions on both sides of the issue. Forrest Park, Confederate Park and Jefferson Davis Park all have our Civil War history as the rationale for their names and themes. Knowledge, reason and prudence, rather than raw emotional reactions, should guide any decisions to rename historical parklands. What categories of information should bear on the deliberative process involved? Where does one start?

In a recent letter to the *Commercial Appeal,* John F. Marshall stated that tourism related to Civil War history alone is a $9 billion a year industry. His letter further notes, "Tennessee is second only to Virginia as the state with the most Civil War battlefields and historical sites." For financial reasons, if no other, he maintains that cash-strapped Memphis should not "destroy our historical sites and sabotage our tourism efforts." Marshall concludes, "Memphians don't have to spend a dime to promote the Civil War sites; the state will do it for us."

In addition to various state agencies promoting tourism broadly, there is a major entity devoted solely to our Civil War– and Reconstruction-era history. According to its website:

> *The Tennessee Civil War National Heritage Area is a federal, state, and local partnership managed by the Center for Historic Preservation at Middle Tennessee State University. The goal of the heritage area is to preserve and interpret the stories, effects, and legacies of the Civil War and Reconstruction in Tennessee. The TCWNHA includes the entire state. [It] is rich in sites, buildings, landscapes and documented sources that tell the stories of the American Civil War and Reconstruction.*
>
> *The TCWNHA is one of the newest of the twenty-three heritage areas. [It is] just beginning to assist Tennessee communities in their programming and tourism efforts and consulting partnership program.*

For more information about this tremendous resource, visit its website at http://histpres.mtsu.edu/tncivwar. Have proponents for changing the names consulted with this entity? Have they consulted with any of our many other historical agencies?

What are other appropriate historical resources? Although the City of Memphis has no municipal historical commission, historian or society, it does have a Landmarks Commission and Memphis Heritage, Inc. to help preserve historical structures. Shelby County has both an official historian and a historical commission but no county historical society. The umbrella historical organization for both Memphis and Shelby County histories is the West Tennessee Historical Society. The Tennessee Historical Commission, the Tennessee Historical Society and the Tennessee Preservation Trust advise on heritage issues from the state level. Such groups deserve our support, and we should employ their expertise in times of doubt or distress. (Virtually all of these entities have websites.)

We need to be very cautious about revising or erasing any of our written, landmark or museum histories, unless something is definitively proved to be factually incorrect. Trendy, short-range revisionism is a very slippery slope that could lead to an Orwellian *1984*-style process of revision and distortion of history to suit evolving political or ideological agendas. Joseph Stalin's

Soviet regime took historical revision to the extreme of eliminating any and all historical references to Tsar Peter the Great, the father of "modern" Russia. Might some folks now demand that we dismantle Andrew Jackson's Hermitage because he was a slave owner and the architect of the Indian removal that resulted in "the Trail of Tears"? Is it an embarrassment that we have Frazee's historic bust of Jackson, which was allegedly defaced by secessionists during the Civil War, in a place of prominence in the Shelby County Courthouse? Where does one stop, short of burning books?

The fact that such questions can actually arise in the twenty-first century testifies to our ongoing need for strong and strongly supported state and local heritage organizations. We should consult them, heed them and give them our moral and financial support.

Local History Buffs Dedicate Historical Marker for the Civil War's Battle of Memphis

At 1:00 p.m. on Friday, June 6, 2008, several local historical groups dedicated a long-overdue historical marker commemorating the June 6, 1862 naval Battle of Memphis. Shelby County Historical Commission chairman Lee Millar presided and, as president of the West Tennessee Historical Society, John Harkins made brief remarks about several levels of significance regarding this naval battle and its outcome.

The text of the new, illustrated marker begins:

> *Atop these bluffs in the early morning hours of June 6, 1862, the citizens of Memphis gathered in excited anticipation as the Confederate River Defense Fleet steamed out into the Mississippi to meet the descending Union Gunboat Fleet. The "cotton-clad" Confederate Fleet, under the command of Captain James E. Montgomery, was comprised of 8 converted wooden paddlewheel steamboats…armed with a total of 18 cannon and protected by "armor" of cotton bales and oak planking.*

The Union fleet, composed of eight heavily armed ironclad warships, commanded by Commodore Charles Henry Davis, and nine speedy, experimental wooden rams, commanded by Colonel Charles Ellet Jr., had the little rebel armada hopelessly out-classed. Accordingly, within ninety minutes the battle was over and the make-do Confederate fleet was gone. Three of its boats were sunk, three ran aground, one was captured and the last escaped south to fight another day. Only one Union ship

The Civil War's naval Battle of Memphis lasted only about ninety minutes, but it was very dramatic (as depicted above) and forever changed the city's social and economic atmosphere. *Courtesy of the Memphis and Shelby County Room, Memphis Public Library.*

The Union's ironclad and battle ram fleet easily demolished the make-do Confederate naval defenses in the Battle of Memphis on June 6, 1862. Union troops occupied the city immediately thereafter. *Courtesy of Special Collections, University of Memphis.*

ran aground, and one other was heavily damaged. Ironically, the single Unionist combatant killed in this action was Colonel Ellet, designer and commander of the victorious U.S. ram fleet. A Confederate sharpshooter mortally wounded him during the fray.

91

The loss of the South's Mississippi River fleet left the city of Memphis completely defenseless. Although Mayor John Park refused to surrender, he conceded that he was powerless to prevent Union occupation. Thus, the Confederacy's fifth-largest city came under Union occupation for the duration of the war; the rest of western Tennessee lay open to Federal troops' occupation; and the Mississippi River was opened to invasion all the way downriver to Vicksburg.

Both the historical marker and the dedication ceremony were cosponsored by the Shelby County Historical Commission, the West Tennessee Historical Society, the Forrest Historical Society and the N.B. Forrest Camp 215, Sons of Confederate Veterans. Participants unveiled the marker, read its text, fired musket salutes and played and sang martial songs from the Civil War era. Following the marker dedication, local historian Alan Doyle paid a brief, slightly belated, 200th birthday tribute to Confederate president Jefferson Davis.

For more details on the Battle of Memphis, please visit Confederate Park and read the marker.

A Victorian Village Christmas Party in 1906

Except for the actual story of Christ's birth, Britain's Victorian era has perhaps had the most profound impact on Americans' perceptions of what Christmas should be. British literature, especially the work of Charles Dickens, is probably most responsible for this phenomenon. At various times, Overton Square and other commercial entities have decorated their exteriors and donned nineteenth-century costumes in efforts to recreate those storied Christmas seasons. Our city's Victorian Village, however, does the most authentic local portrayals of Victorian Christmases.

During the last quarter of the nineteenth century and the first decade of the twentieth century, opulent homes along Adams and Jefferson Avenues were probably at the peak of their prominence and prestige. Their residents were among the city's economic leaders and thus set social trends for contemporary Memphians. Christmas holidays furnished both religious and social highlights for all of the "best" families. And how did such Memphians observe Christmas a century or so ago?

Longtime Woodruff-Fontaine Home devotee Jeanne Crawford refers us to a newspaper article of December 25. This piece informs us:

Places to Find Portions of Our Shared Past

On Christmas Eve, 1906, Elliott, the youngest living son of Noland and Virginia Fontaine, gave an elaborate evening party for 75 of his friends. Elliott was single, and his next oldest brother, Noland Jr. and his wife, Allie, chaperoned the evening affair for the 22-year old.

The next morning's *Commercial Appeal* described the dazzling party as follows:

Seventy-five of the younger society set were entertained last night by Elliott Fontaine at his beautiful and luxurious home on Adams street, Mr. and Mrs. Noland Fontaine, Jr., chaperoning the party.

The hallway was decorated with holly and palms, the stairway wreathed with ropes of greenery, mixed with branches of holly and sprays of red berries. The drawing room was canvassed, the alcove for the musicians banked with palms, and a large bunch of mistletoe hung from the chandelier

Early twentieth-century Memphis was a growing city of the New South, as this 1912 photograph of bustling Main Street, with its rising skyscrapers, illustrates. *Courtesy of the Memphis and Shelby County Room, Memphis Public Library.*

in the center. Holly and red berries mingled with the blaze of lights to make it a beautiful and dazzling ballroom.

The parlor was decorated in the same holiday style with holly, mistletoe and palms, but the dining room was the crowning glory of the evening in the originality of its arrangement. Santa Claus stood in the center, a very life-like and jovial old fellow, and around him were grouped four Christmas trees lighted with candles and decked in proper style. The table was covered with tulle sprinkled with diamond dust and the room was further decorated with holly.

An Oriental den in the rear of the hall proved one of the most attractive spots in the house and was a charming hiding place for Cupid who aimed many a well-directed arrow between dances.

At 12 o'clock a guessing contest was held to discover the number of spices stuck in a pineapple: the lucky guesser among the girls receiving a fleur de lis hat pin set with pearls; among the men, a scarf pin of the same design. Following this a very delicious supper was served, after which dancing by the music of the very excellent band was continued until an early hour of Christmas morning.

Woodruff-Fontaine recreates that atmosphere each year for its visitors between Thanksgiving and the first of the year. For more information, please call (901) 526-1469 or visit the home's website at http://www.woodruff-fontaine.com/.

Shades of History

At Elmwood

Morbid? I think not! Loaded with local history? I know so! Elmwood Cemetery is arguably the most historical spot in the entire Mid-South. Not only does its eighty-acre tract contain the remains of many significant historical figures, but its nonprofit corporation also furnishes staff and resources to help individuals conduct their own research quests. For decades, Elmwood has been helping mid-southerners learn their history and get it right. Elmwood's historian, Jorja (pronounced like "Georgia") Frazier, and Executive Director Kim Caldwell are delighted to aid researchers, whether they are learning about our broader community or are focused mainly on their own family lore. Elmwood brings context and unique informational resources to the search process.

Over a five-year span, *Old Shelby County* provided Memphians with vivid and dramatic renderings of their area's vibrant history. Perhaps its stories will be published again in book form. *Courtesy of* Old Shelby County *magazine.*

Founded in 1852, Elmwood is one of the oldest institutions in the Memphis area. Its beauty and ambiance have led many persons to more profound interest and involvement in the history of our locale. In fact, upon viewing a statue at Elmwood, one man became sufficiently interested in Wade Bolton's story that he researched and wrote a book on the Bolton-Dickens feud. Also, nearly two decades ago, two venerable local history groups nearly got into a tussle over which of them would create a film or video about Elmwood. Feelings ran strong on both sides. For a number of complex reasons, neither group actually undertook the project.

In recent years, however, Elmwood's story has been very well told and retold. Its 1874 handbook, filled with institutional history and biographical sketches of some of its most prominent "residents," has been reprinted. More recently, noted local historian Perre Magness has written a very strong update on the cemetery's history. Her *Elmwood: In the Shadow of the Elms*, with stunning photographs by Murray Riss and an introduction by Shelby Foote, contains more than twelve hundred brief biographical sketches of fascinating individuals. These include Civil War generals and Confederate female spies, slave traders and outlaws, shady ladies and saintly nuns, plus victims of our nation's worst maritime disaster and those of the yellow fever plagues of the 1870s. As Elmwood enthusiasts often observe, "Not everyone here is famous, but everyone has a story."

William (Willy) Bearden, award-winning local videographer, has also captured the essence of Elmwood in his documentary *Elmwood: Reflections of Memphis*. Bearden's video has aired on WKNO, the local PBS affiliate and frequently on the public library's cable channel.

Elmwood is a phenomenon that should interest all Memphis-area history buffs. Elmwood books and videos are available and easily accessible. For more information, please visit www.elmwoodcemetery.org on the Internet. If you do decide to visit, at a minimum, you will want to take a driving tour through Elmwood.

PART V

Twentieth-Century Politics and Government

Crump Reconsidered

Professor Kenneth Jackson and Crump's Manuscripts Collection

In writing about Memphis history, there may be no thornier problem than determining how to treat E.H. Crump and his political organization. On balance, was his long rule good or bad for Memphis? Memphis writers have usually either idolized or villainized Crump, seldom finding any middle ground. In October 2004, reconsideration of Crump's rule and role took place with the commemoration of the fiftieth anniversary of his death and with the Memphis Central Library's Symposium at the opening of the Crump manuscript collection to public use.

Dr. Kenneth T. Jackson, native Memphian, Columbia University professor and renowned urban historian, delivered the symposium's keynote address. Jackson made several brief observations, which included the following: Crump has been the most influential Memphis leader to date. He was honest, efficient, effective and responsive. He was generally a conciliator who created coalitions. He loved Memphis and its people. He exuded sincerity. He generally controlled much of Tennessee's statewide politics. He was among the three most powerful urban bosses in American history. And he was an important figure in the evolution of municipal government in the United States. It is difficult to quarrel with Professor Jackson's assertions.

After establishing his framework, Jackson expressed the hope that the newly available Crump papers would help scholars answer three provocative questions. He asked, rhetorically, whether Crump was good or bad for Memphis, whether he was a racist and whether he was a democrat with a lowercase *d*. Jackson meant to leave his questions open ended, and, to a

Edward Hull Crump Jr. (shown very relaxed here) and his organization dominated Memphis, Shelby County and much of Tennessee politics for most of the early twentieth century. *Courtesy of Special Collections, University of Memphis.*

large extent, he did. However, he did offer some evidence for his listeners' consideration. For example, he asked if there would have even been a sanitation workers' strike in 1968 if Crump's organization had still been in place. On the racist question, of course Crump was a segregationist who saw blacks as inferior. Even so, he held less restrictive racial views than fellow Memphians at that time. Memphis blacks voted, had political influence and had access to patronage and many held fairly good jobs. Admittedly, the police mistreated blacks, but there was much less brutality here than in other southern cities. Moreover, the Crump machine had opposed the Ku Klux Klan in the mid-1920s, denying it political control of the city.

The question of how democratic Memphis was under Crump is much more challenging to answer. There is considerable evidence of the machine's election tampering and some instances of stark intimidation of political foes. On the whole, however, the machine thrived because it had largely ruled with the consent of the governed. Again, now that the 337 boxes of Crump documents are available, some of the numerous questions about the man and the machine should be answered.

Following Dr. Jackson's remarks, several Crump relations told how they had come to the decision to place the collection with the public library. They also related anecdotes of their relationships and memories of their kinsman.

Major figures in (or allied with) the Crump organization rallied at the 1940 Democratic National Convention. They enjoyed dinning at a posh Chicago restaurant owned by a former Memphian. *Courtesy of Special Collections, University of Memphis.*

The program then wound up with panels of local historians discussing Crump's role on the national stage and his place in Memphis history.

For mid-southerners desiring to know more about the Crump era, there is a good bit of published material available on him. Good places for a brief overview would include my own *Metropolis of the American Nile*, Paul Coppock's six hardcover compendiums of his *Commercial Appeal* columns and several articles in the *West Tennessee Historical Society Papers*. Much more comprehensive information and context are available in William D. Miller's *Memphis in the Progressive Era* and *Mr. Crump of Memphis*. David M. Tucker's *Memphis Since Crump*, Robert A. Lanier's *Memphis in the Twenties*, Roger Biles's *Memphis in the Great Depression* and Wayne Dowdy's *Mayor Crump Don't Like It* also contain valuable treatments of Crump and the machine. It is to be hoped, of course, that a major new history of the Crump era will emerge from the historical treasure trove that Crump descendants have made available to researchers. They have given local history a very important manuscripts collection.

Robert A. Tillman, Raconteur Extraordinaire

Over the last two years, I have worked during much of my "off time" on text and illustrations for a new book entitled *Historic Shelby County*. My research included reviewing Robert A. Tillman's recollections of his dealings with the E.H. Crump machine. Bob was a magnificent storyteller, and I heard him hold forth perhaps a dozen times.

A native Mississippian, Bob moved to Memphis after high school, worked as a linotype operator and studied law at night. Intelligent, affable and articulate, he held increasingly important posts in the local typographical union. Because of his strong position within organized labor, Crump's organization recruited him to become part of its team. He moved rapidly up in its ranks. Between 1938 and 1945, he served as an assistant public defender, as Shelby County public defender, as a representative and Shelby County floor leader in the Tennessee General Assembly and as judge of the newly created division IV of general sessions court.

Tillman's assumption that the local judicial system would be apolitical turned out to be misplaced. When he refused to conduct his bench as desired by Crump organization bigwigs, some of them wanted him removed from office. Because of his personal popularity, oratorical skills and labor union connections, however, the machine chose not to run a candidate against him. Instead, the Tennessee legislature simply dissolved his division of general sessions court. Thus, Bob lost his job and became a political and economic pariah. In private practice, few clients would risk engaging him as counsel.

In the 1948 elections, Tillman spoke widely and often on behalf of candidates opposed by the Crump camp. Bob's dramatic, heartfelt speeches probably helped Gordon Browning and Estes Kefauver win their statewide Democratic primary races. Crump's candidates still won in Shelby County by two-to-one margins, but that proved insufficient to decide the outcomes statewide. The machine survived this defeat, but not Crump's death in 1954. Bob returned to public service and frequently regaled listeners with stories of the regime's workings.

A favorite method of firing a "turncoat" went as follows: When an aspiring candidate wanted the machine's support, he had to commit completely to being a team player. To get that support the aspirant had to sign an undated letter of resignation. If he later turned on "his friends," they simply dated his resignation and turned it in to the appropriate office. The "disloyal" official then had to depart or reveal that he had been "bought off" before the election. Game ended!

Robert A. Tillman at his post leading the Shelby delegation in the 1941 session of the Tennessee General Assembly. *Courtesy of the Memphis and Shelby County Room, Memphis Public Library.*

"Big Joe" Brennan's Benign Face on the Crump Organization

Recently, I have been working to help videographers Rob and Pam Cooper redefine their research needs for creating a documentary on the mid-twentieth-century reform elements that pretty much supplanted the E.H. Crump machine in governing Memphis and Shelby County. Their film's primary focus will be on Lucius Burch, Edward Meeman and Edmund Orgill. However, it must also include some assessment of the nature and functioning of the Crump organization. There's the rub. Local old folks and historians alike disagree mightily over whether "the organization" was essentially benign and efficient or corrupt and pernicious. "It just ain't that simple, folks." Organization stalwart J.J. (Big Joe) Brennan's career provides an example of why. Quoting freely from his obituary articles appearing in the local newspapers of February 20, 1945, serves to illustrate this point.

"Genial Joe" Brennan was a second-tier leader in the Crump organization. News of his death "brought expressions of honest regret from an extraordinarily wide and varied range of Memphians." Their condolences gave "an accurate estimate of the unusually great number of ways in which [Joe] had effectively busied himself to the end that Memphis might be a better city and its people happier." Over the decades, Joe had held many offices of

public trust and responsibility. In the discharge of his duties, he never lost sight of the basic interests of the people of the community and he served faithfully and well. As a member of the Park Commission, and later as its chairman, he was especially instrumental in building up the zoo and in seeing that wading pools and other facilities for children were provided.

During all his years in Memphis, there was hardly any worthy cause that did not have the benefit of Joe Brennan's interest, energy and enthusiasm. He was a prime player in the Goodfellow movement that provides cheer at Christmas for needy children, and it was typical of him that he found vast pleasure in that enterprise. He was an active member of the Kiwanis Club, served as its president and furthered its activities ably. He aided substantially in the cause of clean sports. In fact, Joe Brennan concerned himself with a very remarkable variety of undertakings that resulted in good for Memphis, and to them all he brought a ready smile, a genuine kindliness and a friendliness that added immeasurably to the values of what he did. Joe Brennan yearned for human companionship, and few men anywhere have ever been blessed with so many friends. Neither creed nor class raised any barriers against friendship with Joe Brennan.

Brennan headed the city's annual Community Fund drive for eleven straight years, "going over the top" in exceeding its goal each year. He was a good businessman, a splendid organizer and a top salesman. He attended everything of an athletic nature that he could: prep football, bowling, boxing and basketball contests. He also brought top-flight college football games to Memphis. Joe "was a fair man and a fine man." He did as much or more good behind the scenes as he did in the limelight.

Brennan's list of honorary pallbearers' reads like a who's who of local politics. It includes E.H. Crump, Senator Kenneth McKellar, Representative Cliff Davis, Mayor Walter Chandler, all of the Memphis and Shelby County commissioners and all of the department heads of LG&W Division. Joe's posthumous honors include his induction into both the Park Commission and Christian Brothers High School Halls of Fame. The Park Commission also christened a nineteen-acre park and playground in East Memphis, the J.J. Brennan Park.

With unwavering support from men like Joe Brennan, it becomes a little easier to understand why so many Memphians cheerfully supported the Crump machine, despite political abuses associated with the machine's uses of its raw political power.

Henry Loeb

A Snapshot in Time and Transition

The last time I saw Henry Loeb was in the autumn of 1991 at "his" Dutch Treat Luncheon in the ballroom at the Wilson World Hotel near American Way. Mayor-elect Willie Herenton was the guest speaker. The luncheon's very conservative regulars had been certain that Dick Hackett would be reelected by a fairly comfortable margin. Consequently, they had asked luncheon director Charlie Peete to invite the winner of the mayor's contest to be their next speaker. Because of Herenton's "upset" victory, there was a huge turnout for the program. The gloom and angst of the regular attendees was more than offset by the elation of the many African Americans attending the Loeb luncheon for the first time.

A few of the tables, like ours, were racially integrated, but most were self-segregated. I don't remember a whole lot of what was said beyond the polite chitchat at our table. Mayor Herenton made some conciliatory remarks about his vision for the city and his desire to be mayor for all of the people of Memphis. Audience reaction was somewhat mixed, based on respective ideological and/or racial identifications.

Mayor Henry Loeb (above in shirtsleeves) campaigned tirelessly and cheerfully. Initially, he was popular with both black and white Memphians. The 1968 sanitation workers' strike drastically changed that status. *Courtesy of Special Collections, University of Memphis.*

Then, suddenly, former mayor Henry Loeb was at the speaker's platform and offering his congratulations and good wishes to Dr. Herenton. Loeb, who had been stricken by a stroke, had made the trek over from Forrest City, Arkansas, for the occasion. What a wonderful symbol of our system and its tradition of peaceful transitions of power from one highly partisan group to another! Those two towering men stood there, wringing each others' mitts in a four-handed clasp, with warmth and joy on both their faces. Attendees of both races filled the ballroom with a thunderous ovation. Loeb tried to address some remarks to the audience, but his speech was very much impaired and his words badly garbled. The rest of the day was anticlimactic.

As one of the historians who chronicles our city's past, I have always wanted a picture of that transcending moment in our community's history. As far as I am aware, no one photographed that event. If a photo of it does exist, I hope that its owner will make arrangements to let that image be copied for the reference collections of Memphis Public Library and/or the University of Memphis Special Collections.

As Memphis and Shelby County archivist in the early 1980s, I had supervised the processing of Henry Loeb's administrative files. Working with those documents made me quite familiar with the inner workings of his office. Both Loeb's gesture at the luncheon and my close-up knowledge of his actions as mayor have given me the impression that both scholars and the media have given Henry Loeb a pretty "bum rap." I hope to do additional research and writing on Mayor Loeb for future publication in the *Best Times*.

Mother Jones's Memphis Connection

Perhaps it was merely courtroom hyperbole when, in 1902, a U.S. district attorney reportedly called her "the most dangerous woman in America," but perhaps not. Certainly her pink cheeks, white hair, warm smile and conventional dress seemed at odds with such an accusation. Irrespective, Mary Harris Jones "had come a long way" from her days as a teacher, dressmaker, wife and mother. She had grown into one of the most doctrinaire socialists in the American labor movement, and she had become universally known as "Mother Jones." At the roots of her dramatic transformation lies a horrible story set in Memphis, but one for which we have only skimpy evidence.

Mary encountered a great deal of tragedy in her long life. She was born in Cork County, Ireland, in 1837. Within less than a decade, the Great Famine struck, and her father and oldest brother immigrated to Canada to work at railway construction. They soon brought over the rest of the family, and in Toronto, Mary became well schooled in the context of those times. After teaching in Michigan and working briefly as a dressmaker in Chicago, she came to Memphis in 1860. Here, too, the twenty-three-year-old woman taught briefly, before meeting and marrying an Irish-born iron molder named George Jones. As a skilled metal worker, George was well paid, and there are no indications that Mary continued teaching. Even after the city fell into Union hands in 1862, their lives were not greatly disrupted. Mary bore four children, and the family lived in the Pinch area, near the banks of pestilential Bayou Gayoso. The Jones family survived the Civil War and the Memphis race riot of 1866, but peace also brought major economic dislocations. Foundries were consolidated or shut down, and George was among the three-fourths of American molders who became unemployed in 1867. The Joneses had not recovered from this blow when the yellow fever epidemic of 1867 struck Memphis. The Pinch area was hardest hit, and Mary wrote briefly in her *Autobiography* decades later:

Across the street from me, ten persons lay dead from the plague. The dead surrounded us. They were buried at night quickly and without ceremony. All about my house I could hear weeping and cries of delirium. One by one my little children sickened and died. I washed their little bodies and got them ready for burial. My husband caught the fever and died. I sat alone through nights of grief. No one came to me. No one could. Other homes were as stricken as mine. All day long, all night long, I heard the grating of the wheels of the death cart.

The local iron molders' union buried George with honors, and Mary helped to nurse victims in the stricken city until a heavy frost ended the plague. Thereafter, she returned to Chicago and to dressmaking, surviving that city's great fire of 1871.

According to biographer Elliott J. Gorn, however, it was in Memphis that Mary witnessed how greed caused some men to reduce others to slavery. In Memphis, too, she saw armies come to liberate the slaves from bondage. Here she witnessed the explosive mix of racial hatred and class. In Memphis, she first became familiar with the American labor movement and thought about what solidarity meant for people like herself. And in Memphis, she was called "Mother," a title she would not hear again for thirty years.

As Gorn indicates, Mary did not emerge as Mother Jones and become a national figure until long after she left Memphis. Much of her new persona she simply created from whole cloth (pun noted). Her fine-tuned image, however, helped her to become an extraordinarily effective labor organizer and agitator. Indeed, by 1902, she was influential enough to be thought of as a genuine danger to American capitalism.

The Consolidation Issue

The 1967–68 changes in Memphis's government were actually important countywide because progressive political elements were still hoping and working for consolidation of city and county governments. Ultimately, three referenda were held, and the initiative failed in each instance. On the second effort, a majority of Shelby Countians voted to consolidate. However, a provision of the state constitution required a majority vote both inside the major city *and* in the areas outside that city. In this instance, a majority of residents outside the city voted no. This constitutional wrinkle had been the handiwork of Ellen Davies Rodgers. Mrs. Rodgers, owning a significant plantation near Bartlett, Tennessee, had been an ardent Crump

Early in the post-Crump era, reform-minded leaders Jack Ramsay, Bruce Jordan and Dan Mitchell campaigned for office with speaker trucks. They advocated consolidated city-county government and greater efficiency. *Courtesy of Special Collections, University of Memphis.*

supporter, and she was an equally ardent and effective advocate for rural Shelby Countians. She worked to ensure that rural interests would not be subordinated to urban desires—and she prevailed.

In an effort to make the city and county governmental systems more compatible and to facilitate consolidation at some point in the future, the reformers made the new county government as parallel to the city government as they could. Commission chairman Jack Ramsay and his fellow commissioners supported the new structure for county government, as, ultimately, did the county court chairman Charles W. Baker.

Paralleling the structures of Memphis and Shelby County governments did not facilitate consolidation, however. Several considerations have defeated all further efforts at consolidation well into the twenty-first century. These include, but are not limited to, economics, demographics and perceptions of the relative strengths of the Memphis and Shelby County school systems. Initially, Memphis's African American leaders were opposed to consolidation and blanket annexations because those measures would dilute their growing numbers and accompanying political power. Most individuals living outside of Memphis, including those within the county's other municipalities, did not want to be brought under Memphis's control because it would mean higher property and sales taxes for them. Finally, with forced busing to achieve racial balances in the city's school system, county residents did not want to have their children required to attend schools that they viewed as markedly inferior and much more dangerous. In an ironic twist, with shifting demographics, African Americans became the majority ethnic group in both the city and county. Once consolidation would no longer postpone black control of local governments, black leaders wanted to annex and/or consolidate with outlying areas. Many blacks also wanted consolidation of the two school systems, since county schools consistently got much higher ratings for academic effectiveness.

As of this writing, neither consolidation of governments nor school systems has taken place. However, in efforts to cut costs over time, many other functions of city and county governments have been consolidated or merged. Joint agencies, such as Planning and Development, the criminal justice system and the juvenile court system, have become functionally united. In yet another reversal of trends, however, some of the previously begun departmental consolidations have started breaking down. For instance, public libraries in the outlying Shelby County cities and towns have withdrawn from the once-consolidated Memphis/Shelby County library system. Also, the Memphis Police Department has unilaterally withdrawn from some of its consolidated functions, working with the Shelby County Sheriff's Department. It remains to be seen whether centrifugal or centripetal forces will prevail.

Until recently, observers and critics have painted the proposed merger of local governments as a near panacea for solving most of the area's problems. In February 2007, however, Tom Jones (former public affairs officer for Shelby County and currently an associate for the syndicated radio program *Smart City*) published a feature in *Memphis* magazine challenging that bit of conventional wisdom. He stated flatly, "Merging city and county governments won't fix anything. Other cities figured that out years ago." Arguing that most discussion of the matter generated more myths than facts, Jones mustered a few sobering facts himself. His analysis points out that only 35 of America's 3,141 counties have consolidated into "metro governments" with their primary cities. Moreover, only nine of the nation's one hundred largest cities have merged their city and county governments.

Twentieth-Century Politics and Government

In Tennessee, of twenty referenda to create metro governments since 1958, only three have passed. Nashville/Davidson has been the only major urban center to do so, with the other three largest cities rejecting consolidation in multiple referenda. Although many Nashvillians sang the praises of their consolidation a quarter century ago, some are now much less enthusiastic about having taken that step.

A final irony rests in a commonly held perception that, under the Crump regime, Memphis had had a de facto consolidated local government over most of the early twentieth century. The same group of people, irrespective of whether they held office, had made the decisions for both city and county governments. For all of its obvious cronyism and uses of intimidation, the machine had provided relatively popular, inexpensive, honest and efficient local government services.

Most elements of this essay have appeared in Historic Shelby County *and are reprinted here by permission of the Historical Publishing Network.*

PART VI

Cultural Aspects of Memphis History

May (and Its Festivals) in Memphis

If we Memphians could agree on when our community was founded, and if we were inclined to celebrate its founding, we should observe our origins during the month of May. In May 1795, Manuel Gayoso received Chickasaw permission and began building Fort San Fernando on the bluffs. Construction of that fort began the ongoing habitation on what is now Memphis. In May 1819, M.B. Winchester and William Lawrence surveyed the Memphis city streets and began distributing city lots. The following May, the Shelby County government began its operations in the town of Memphis. Municipal government for Memphis did not surface until March 1827, but by then, the actual community was already at least a generation old.

Even though we do not annually celebrate our city's founding, May in Memphis has always been our best time for festivals. By 1860, our city's German immigrants had established *Mai Feste*. Over the next half century they celebrated each May with parades, picnics, music and various other expressions of their ethnicity and culture. These included but were not limited to speeches (usually in German *and* English), militia company marching, fencing, gymnasts' exhibitions, shooting contests, tenpins and many other kinds of games. Their activities were often held in Estival Park and were sponsored by a coalition of Germanic groups, especially the local Teutonia Society. A Memphis newspaper described the 1874 *Mai Feste* parade as having elaborate floats traversing Main Street south from Market Square. The Queen of the May wore a white dress adorned with golden spangles and a gold crown with diamonds. Little maidens, also dressed in white and wreathed in roses, accompanied her.

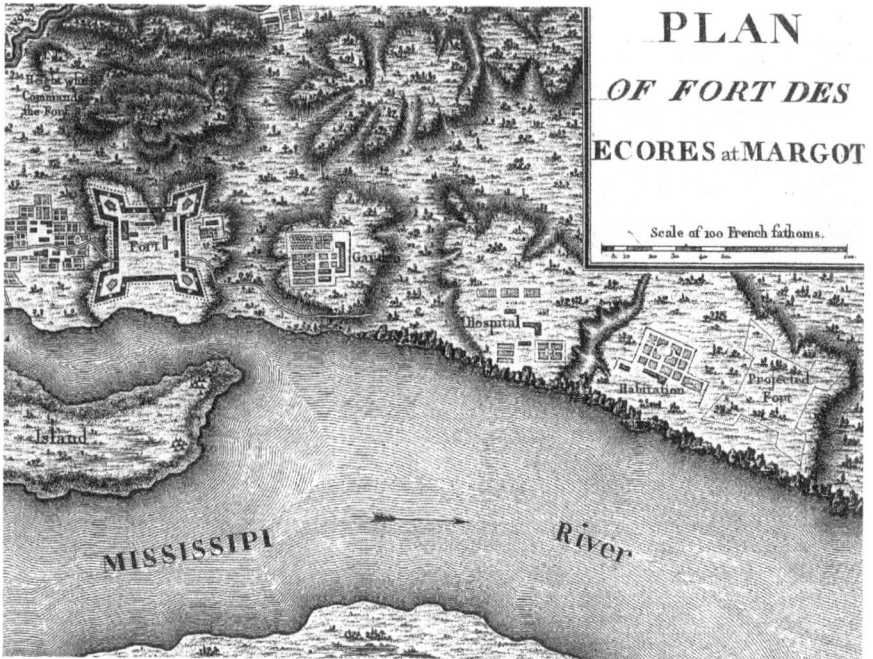

PLAN

OF FORT DES

ECORES at MARGOT

Scale of 100 French fathoms.

In May 1795, Spanish troops built and occupied Fort San Fernando de las Barrancas, about where the Memphis Pyramid stands today. Continuous occupation of the site dates from that time. *Courtesy of Special Collections, University of Memphis.*

Several sources give 1909 as the last year in which German Memphians observed *Mai Feste*. That year, Dr. William J. Oswald's mother, Marie Feller, was the May Queen. Certainly, during World War I, Germanic culture became very unpopular in America, and local *Mai Feste* observances died out.

Memphians doubtlessly "roared" with the rest of the nation during the 1920s, but not until the economically striated 1930s did they return to celebrating a May festival. In its first year, Cotton Carnival was held in early March, but the cold, wet weather inspired organizers to schedule it for May thereafter. Over the years, the carnival's initial three days of celebration expanded to ten. Participation cut across most socioeconomic segments of the city's white population. Various service and social groups were especially involved. The Mid-South's public and private schools took part in children's parades on Main Street and children's balls at Crump Stadium. African Americans, so essential to the region's cotton production, quickly initiated their parallel Cotton Makers' Jubilee. Over recent decades, however, the carnival has been racially integrated.

Public and private schools furnished "royalty" to represent them in annual Cotton Carnival observances. In 1952, John Harkins, Rosemarie Stevens, Charlie Jester and Kay Gardner represented St. Anne School.

As America approached its bicentennial, Memphis's calendar of events for May became crowded with items unrelated to the carnival. Many city boosters wanted to draw national and international attention to the city for the entire month of May. In 1973, under the leadership of Allen Morgan and Thomas Batchelor, they formed the Memphis in May (MIM) Society.

German Americans' *Mai Feste* was a very significant cultural event in late nineteenth and early twentieth centuries, as are twenty-first-century Memphis May events. *Courtesy of Dr. William J. Oswald.*

By 1976, MIM was promoting more than one hundred local events. These included colorful hot-air balloon rallies, Music Fest, the Danny Thomas Golf Classic, the St. Jude Shower of Stars, the Metropolitan Opera, World Championship Barbeque Contests, the Sunset Symphonies and many dozens more. Of course, honoring a guest country, as with Ireland this year, has been key to sustaining the festival's variety and to expanding our commercial and cultural connections around the world. Volunteers initially staged most of the MIM events, but over the decades the festival has become more professional and more commercialized. During that time, Memphis in May became such a dominant social phenomenon that the carnival has moved most of its official activities to early June.

Doubtlessly, Memphis in May, too, will build more traditions and legends in future years and continue making itself central to our city's most vital social interactions. It would probably be a wise and popular move for MIM to add a Founder's Day to its many observances.

What They Say About the Irish

Later this spring, Memphis in May will honor Ireland as our guest country. Certainly it is fitting to finally honor the Emerald Isle. After all, our "first Memphian" was arguably an Irish immigrant. Moreover, our most notable schoolmaster immigrated from Ireland; our best-known bard (Walter Malone, "Opportunity") was of Irish descent; and the Irish were the city's largest ethnic minority between the 1850s and about 1890. Finally, as late as the 1990 census, about 160,000 Shelby Countians identified themselves as Irish-Americans, composing our area's second-largest ethnic group.

Irishman "Paddy" Meagher may well have been the earliest "permanent" settler on the site of Memphis. Meagher was here during the Revolutionary War; he was either still here or back here under the Spanish in 1795–97; and he remained here until his death in the 1820s. As one of our earliest settlers, Meagher sold goods to passing riverboats and owned and operated the legendary Bell Tavern. Professor James Roper debunked many of the Meagher myths, but Paddy remains a legendary founder of our community.

Within a decade of Meagher's death, Irish-born schoolmaster Eugene Magevney was in Memphis seeking and ultimately finding his fortune. Probably the best known of our city's nineteenth-century Irish immigrants, Magevney sponsored the Dominican Order's religious presence here and had a major role in the founding of St. Peter's Church and St. Agnes Academy. He was also the person most responsible for starting the city's public school system in the late 1840s. Magevney served on the city council until his death in the yellow fever epidemic of 1873. His descendants donated his 1830s clapboard-covered log house at 198 Adams Avenue to Memphis as a museum.

Memphis's Irish-American community was just starting to control local politics when the devastating yellow fever epidemics of the 1870s struck. The plague took a particularly brutal toll on the city's Gaels: the vast majority of Memphis's five thousand deaths in the 1878 epidemic were Irish. The heroism of the largely Irish Catholic priests and nuns of this era is also legendary.

Irish orphans of the Civil War and yellow fever eras made up part of the city's notorious Mackerel Brigade of scavenging street urchins. Their antics may have helped motivate the operations of St. Peter's Orphanage, which hosted more than a century of Memphis Fourth of July charity picnics and political gatherings.

Paddy Meagher's legendary Bell Tavern dated from the early 1820s and survived into the early twentieth century. Contrary to popular myth, the city was not laid out there. *Courtesy of Special Collections, University of Memphis.*

Irish citizens generated perhaps a dozen or more ethnic fraternal organizations into the late nineteenth century. With the city's unhealthy reputation, however, Memphis attracted few new immigrants after 1880. As local Irish-Americans assimilated and intermarried with other ethnic groups, their clubs also declined. By the late 1920s, the Ancient Order of Hibernians gave way to the Irish Society of Memphis, which, like most local social organizations of the time, was also an arm of the Crump machine. In fact, a number of Crump's stalwarts were ethnically Irish, notably Roxie Rice, Charles Bryan, John T. "Buddy" Dwyer, Joe Boyle, Samuel O. Bates, Edward Barry, Joe Brennan and Ed English. Of course, not every Irish Memphian supported the Crump machine. C.P.J. Mooney, the *Commercial Appeal*'s Pulitzer Prize–winning editor, became and remained one of Crump's foremost opponents.

The Memphis Irish Society thrived for about sixty years. In the late 1980s, under the auspices of the Memphis International Heritage Commission (IHC), it sponsored three grand ethnic exhibits and receptions in city hall. In the 1990s, however, both the Irish Society and the IHC wilted away.

Those wanting to read about the history of the Memphis Irish should check the *WTHS Papers*, volumes 6, 45 and 50, for works by William Stanton, Joe Brady and Darrell B. Uselton, respectively. Also, see "Like a Plague of Locusts"

Cultural Aspects of Memphis History

by Kathleen Berkeley and the vignettes of Paul R. Coppock in his six volumes of Memphis history. For researchers, the University of Memphis Libraries Special Collections Department has the papers of the Memphis Irish Society.

Histories of Temple Israel and the Annunciation Greek Orthodox Church

Recently, this column made reference to Judge John Getz having written a history of St. Brigid Catholic Church. Local historians often overlook such histories of religious congregations, although they frequently contain marvelous historical tidbits offered in no other readily available sources. (For example, Ellen Davies Rodgers's *The Holy Innocence* contains 115 pages of excerpts from the diaries of Captain Kenneth Garrett, a turn-of-the-twentieth-century stalwart of the community that became Arlington, Tennessee.) Rarely read outside of their own circles of faith, such histories are usually under appreciated and under used. Admittedly, the quality of such historical studies may be uneven. But many such histories, although usually commissioned and published by their respective congregations, often contain highly professional research, writing, design and production.

Two such religious communities have recently published excellent histories as hardcover books. These two treatments are Judy G. Ringel's *Children of Israel—The Story of Temple Israel, Memphis Tennessee: 1854–2004* and *Beyond Ellis Island—The Memphis Greeks: Our Faith and Our Heritage* by Catherine Mazas Hatzigeorgiou, Cathe Hetos Skefos and Sophie Makris Sousoulas. Both books are well written, lavishly illustrated and beautifully designed and printed. More importantly, each book projects a strong element of its congregation's ethnic, as well as its religious, heritage. It is probable that language, culture, food, et cetera, have helped their respective groups sustain tighter bonds of community than is generally the case in ethnically broader-based denominations. As the best of such works frequently do, theses two books have strong contextual elements that make them interesting, readable and valuable beyond their central purposes.

The Israel and Annunciation histories also interest me, at least in part, because of their coverage of two of my favorite local icons: Rabbi James A. Wax and Father Nicholas L. Vieron. Although I have had only a brushing personal acquaintance with these men, both appeared for many years on my favorite local television program, *What Is Your Faith?* Wax and Vieron were outstanding among a panel of eight or ten prominent local ministers. The group responded to viewers' questions about nearly anything related to religious perspectives. With wit and wisdom, Vieron and Wax projected a generosity of spirit and ecumenical inclusion that other panelists sometimes seemed to lack. Moreover, their knowledge of the original languages of the scriptures made their insights particularly valuable.

Wax and Vieron, apparently close personal friends, were also community leaders well beyond the bounds of their own congregations. Active in efforts to secure civil justice for local African Americans, they helped make local history. Furthermore, both men seem to just keep on giving. As his health declined, the late Rabbi Wax donated his personal research materials to the public library for use by future scholars. Father Vieron, now retired, continues to teach Memphians an annual crash course in Greek language and culture, the roots of our Western heritage.

Of course, the Temple Israel and Annunciation books are broader, richer institutional histories shedding light on much more than just two of my personal heroes. Moreover, they are only two of numerous congregational and denominational histories available for the Memphis area.

Probably the earliest local congregation to have published its history is Big Creek Baptist Church, which may have been founded prior to the Chickasaw Cession in 1819. Paul T. Hicks's *History of First Methodist Church—Memphis, Tennessee: 1826–1900* seems to come next in time, followed by Ellen Davies Rodgers's *The Great Book—Calvary Protestant Episcopal Church: 1832–1972.* There are probably dozens of other religious community histories of our area available to be encountered and savored by local history lovers. For additional information on such works, visit the Tennessee Genealogical Society's website at www.wdbj.net/shelby/bibliography/index3.html, or call (901) 754-4300.

Memphis YMCA Celebrates
Its 150th Anniversary

The famous eighteenth-century French philosopher and social critic Voltaire once described Europe's Holy Roman Empire as neither holy, nor Roman nor an empire. Institutions evolve. The Memphis area's Young Men's Christian Association is no longer limited to the young, to males or even to Christians, although it continues to promote Christian principles. The YMCA has been an invaluable asset to Memphis over many decades, and its story deserves to be told.

Sir George Williams and about a dozen friends founded the YMCA in London in 1844, in an effort to combat the unhealthy social conditions generated by England's Industrial Revolution. Rural lads migrating to

Cultural Aspects of Memphis History

Britain's manufacturing and commercial centers often proved vulnerable to new temptations in the urban environment. Without wholesome activities at hand, such youths were drawn to grog houses, gambling houses and houses of prostitution. Williams's evangelical Protestant group helped the boys to combat idleness and decadence by promoting Bible classes and prayer meetings. Perhaps surprisingly, this movement proved so popular that within a dozen years, Britain had twenty-four such associations with a membership of about three thousand young men. Moreover, the movement had also spread to population centers in seven countries, including the United States. The Y's more than four hundred associations had more than thirty thousand members. By 1855, five young Memphians had initiated our local chapter.

The outbreak of the American Civil War in 1861 initially paralyzed the nation's YMCA movement, but the institution quickly adapted to new circumstances. It became a civilian volunteer organization dedicated to the well-being of prisoners of war and other military servicemen. In Memphis, however, war, Union occupation, Reconstruction and three horrendous bouts of yellow fever caused a suspension of YMCA activities.

When the Memphis YMCA resumed its work in 1883, it occupied a rented room over a downtown store. The group installed a few simple pieces of furniture and a modest library. Although little is known of the Y's activities between 1883 and about 1907, the leadership of John R. Pepper and Thomas B. King kept the association viable. In 1907, the Memphis Y moved toward acquiring first-rate facilities. It launched a capital campaign, purchased land at Fourth and Madison and announced plans to construct a $200,000 building on the site. The Y's efforts yielded a magnificent seven-story building, which officials dedicated with great fanfare on October 27, 1909. In addition to Governor Malcolm Patterson and governors from numerous other states, President William Howard Taft and much of the city's population gathered to mark the occasion.

Although the Y has stayed true to its mission, advancing its members in spirit, mind and body, the modalities of service and the nature of its membership have evolved markedly over the last century. During the First World War, the Y became deeply involved in furnishing relief for suffering Europeans and in sending aid to the American Expeditionary Forces. During World War II, the Y joined with other organizations to form the United Service Organizations (USO), which supplied entertainment, social services and spiritual guidance to American servicemen around the globe.

With the support of its members and the donations of local philanthropists, the Memphis-area Y has grown phenomenally in the postwar era. It has met a broad spectrum of community needs, many of them firsts for our area.

Sitting president William Howard Taft (the mustached man in the front, just left of center) headlined the list of dignitaries in dedicating the palatial 1910 YMCA building in downtown Memphis. *Courtesy of Special Collections, University of Memphis.*

Over the last century, it has operated camps at Mammoth Springs, Arkansas, and Pickwick Lake. It has provided exercise facilities, gymnasiums (the Y was instrumental in the founding of both basketball and volleyball), tennis and racquetball courts, indoor and outdoor swimming pools, affordable lodging (especially for servicemen), day camps during the summers, athletic instruction, early intervention programs and so much more.

Our area's thirteen YMCA operations are very much family services organizations. They have impressive facilities, especially the magnificently renovated downtown (Louis T. Fogelman) branch, the Collierville Branch and the newest branch at Olive Branch, Mississippi. In October 2005, the Memphis-area YMCA branches celebrated the 150th anniversary of their founding. They held a Black-Tie Gala on Saturday, October 29, at the Peabody. Dinner and dancing was to swing music of the big band era. Fittingly, tickets were $150 per person.

Paul Flowers and the Mid-South Writers' Association

The bad news is that I am leaving full-time teaching this summer. The good news is that I will serve as Memphis University School's first writer in residence next year. Since I will be focusing much more on research and writing, I have (again) become an active member of the Mid-South Writers' Association (MSWA).

MSWA is a valuable and venerable institution. It was the brainchild of local journalist Paul A. Flowers, presumably in the 1960s or '70s. Paul was apparently a larger-than-life figure in more ways than one. He became famous in our region for his Falstaffian girth and wit, for wearing a huge variety of dramatic hats, for chomping large cigars, for hosting an enormous array of literati and glitterati friends and acquaintances in his columns and for being something of a curmudgeon. He was generally admired, often beloved and a very interesting eccentric.

Paul had a fascinating career in journalism and as an adjunct college instructor, teaching political science, journalism and creative writing at a half dozen colleges. He got off to a slow academic start, however, having had difficulties in high school and in his early attempts at college. During the late 1920s and 1930s, he relocated a lot, working at newspapers in various parts of the country and overcoming a tendency toward misanthropy. He later buckled down and earned bachelor's and master's degrees at Ohio State and a doctorate at Erskine College.

In 1943, Flowers became a fixture at the *Commercial Appeal*, writing his daily "Greenhouse" column and editing the paper's weekly book page. Referred to by colleagues as "the Professor," and sometimes "the plump pundit," he published light verse and whatever miscellaneous prose happened to strike his fancy. Many of his columns were compiled and reprinted annually in booklet form, called *Greenhouse Books*. Of his work, University of Tennessee president Andy Holt wrote:

Paul Flowers served for decades as book editor and literary critic at the *Commercial Appeal*, taught creative writing at the college level and founded the Mid-South Writers' Association. *Courtesy of Memphis University School Archives.*

With his enormous audience of regular readers [Paul] has had as much influence upon the literary education of the people in the Mid-South as any other single individual in that region...He is nationally recognized as an authority on Southern literature and folklore, and is in great demand as a book reviewer, speaker, critic, and judge of literary works.

All of that being said, Paul Flowers's most enduring legacy seems to be the Mid-South Writers' Association. This group grew out of one of his creative writing classes and initially met in his home. Nearly a quarter of a century after his demise, the group is still helping turn aspirants into writers. Members of MSWA now meet monthly at MUS to read and critique one another's work, gingerly helping future writers hone their skills and build their confidence.

For more information on MSWA, go online to http://midsouthwriters.blogspot.com.

Memphis Music Before the Blues

The programs offered through the West Tennessee Historical Society continue to provide joy, artistry and understanding for those who make time to attend. Certainly, the society's December meeting fit that bill. Professor Tim Sharp, dean of fine arts at Rhodes College, delighted and informed society members with information, samples of music and images illustrative of the Bluff City's leadership in music during the nineteenth century.

Working with students from the Rhodes Institute for Regional Studies and drawing on the resources of the University of Memphis, the Memphis Public Library and private family collections, Dr. Sharp and his students gathered information on many local musicians, conductors and composers. They researched their topic "until the story began to take shape as a book." That book, *Memphis Music Before the Blues,* was released by Arcadia Publishing in 2007 and provides the heart of Sharp's oral presentations.

There is a great deal for even the seasoned student of Memphis history to learn about our musical roots. Our city's position on the Mississippi River was a significant factor in it becoming a music center. The river was a major transportation artery, and steamboats carried musical groups up- and downriver and used their talents to entertain passengers en route. Although the Italians, Germans, Irish and African Americans were all significant contributors, the German immigrants were especially strong in their contributions to the city's formal music.

Cultural Aspects of Memphis History

Professor Sharp enlivened his lecture with taped snippets and his own live strumming of nineteenth-century music. He was very generous in taking and responding to questions from the audience before, during and following his lecture. Some of the program's rapt attendees were descended from the city's nineteenth-century musical movers and shakers. One member even spotted his wife in a photograph of one of the Goodwyn Institute concerts. During the very lively question and answer session following Sharp's remarks, he took copious notes on information provided by audience comments. The interest of a few participants was such that their discussion with Sharp continued in the parking lot for perhaps an hour after the meeting had adjourned.

Arcadia Publishing has generated at least a dozen books on Mid-South history over recent years. Local history fans are aware that Arcadia's formulaic format is strongest in the number, quality and variety of its images. The lavish use of tickets, sheet music, programs and photographs make Sharp's book a visual delight. Its images and information span the spectrum from Jenny Lind's tour stop here to the very plebian minstrel shows. It helps fill a major gap in our city's cultural history.

Memphis Music Before the Blues is available in local bookstores.

Judge John Brennan Getz (1934–2005)

A Personal Reminiscence

Judge Getz loved history! He especially loved local and nineteenth-century history. His death in December 2005 cost local history one of its most earnest students, most devoted contributors and best resources. John's interest and expertise were particularly strong on our municipal history, Shelby County history, Irish-American history, Catholic Church history, Civil War history, yellow fever history and the history of the bench and bar. He most enjoyed shedding light on topics that brought two or more of his special interests together. He loved the eloquence and the elegance of nineteenth-century historians' prose, and he collected a fine personal library of local lore.

John's death has been a great personal loss for me, as well. We became friends in the early 1950s, when he was schoolmates and teammates at Christian Brothers College with my older brothers. He was a frequent guest in our home and a mentor to my "generation" (four years younger) of pre-high schoolers. After his graduation, John served a tour of duty in the marine corps, mainly in Korea. Soon after he returned to civilian life, I departed for nearly a decade of service in the navy. We encountered each

Judge John B. Getz contributed a great deal to Memphis-area history, focusing his efforts primarily on the areas of Catholic Church, Civil War, Irish, legal and yellow fever history. *Courtesy of Joseph Getz.*

other rarely but warmly through the 1960s and '70s. About 1980, however, we became serious comrades in Clio's legions. John came to "my" City/County Archives to do historical research, and we discovered our mutual fascination with local history.

Getz came to his appreciation for local history almost by osmosis. His great-grandfather, police captain John Brennan, had served in local government and was a stalwart of John T. Walsh's North Memphis political organization. His grandfather, John Joseph "Big Joe" Brennan, was a mainstay of the Crump machine and served as the vice-president of Memphis Light, Gas & Water (municipally owned utilities) Division, chairman of the Memphis Park Commission and a major figure in the Irish Society, the Goodfellows and other civic and charitable organizations. John grew up with history being made all around him. No doubt, those early influences also gave him leanings toward public service and law enforcement. Moreover, his own work as sheriff's deputy, private attorney, assistant public defender, city court judge and general sessions judge all served to enhance his interest in and his knowledge of Memphis-area history.

John lent his time and talents to a number of local history organizations and agencies, including the West Tennessee Historical Society (serving on the board over most of the last twenty years), and the Descendants of Early Settlers of Shelby County (serving as president for four years in the early 1990s). He worked as institutional historian for both the Memphis Irish Society and St. Peter's Catholic Church and served as a board member of the Davies Manor Association. He served on the Shelby County Historical Commission and on the judicial committee for the restorations of the Shelby County Courthouse and Archives Buildings. He researched, wrote and published in the areas of legal history, including a history of the general sessions courts, a history of the Archibald Wright family and a history of the Shelby County Attorney General's Office. He also did a thorough study of St. Brigid's Catholic Church. Much of John's other work appeared as book reviews and edited documents in the *West Tennessee Historical Society Papers*.

Getz greatly enjoyed talking about our history. He served as historical consultant and commentator on cable television programs and on WKNO's Memphis history series. He pulled together a small Dutch-treat luncheon and history discussion group, audio taping our conversations and later giving us transcriptions.

John and I aided and abetted each other in numerous ways in our local history pursuits. We vetted each other's manuscripts, shared our local history images and attended scores of history meetings together. John usually worked behind the scenes to get things done. He joyfully and enthusiastically shared his knowledge and views, caring little who got credit for ensuing achievements. His aid in gathering illustrations was invaluable to both my Memphis and MUS histories. In our research and writing, and in our various organizational endeavors, Getz and I often seemed metaphorically joined at the hip. John Getz was my great, good friend, but he was even more so a friend to Mid-South history. We local history buffs will all suffer now, trying to get along without him.

ABOUT THE AUTHOR

D r. John E. Harkins and his wife, Georgia, are both fifth-generation Memphians with decades-long, passionate commitments to Memphis-area history and to institutions serving that history. John taught history for thirty-plus years, with more than twenty-five of those years being at Memphis University School. He has written dozens of articles on Mid-South history and three highly regarded books on Memphis and Shelby County topics. These include *Metropolis of the American Nile, MUS Century Book* and *Historic Shelby County.* The first two of these have also been republished in revised editions.

By way of preparation in local history, John served six years as Memphis and Shelby County archivist, eight years on the Tennessee Public Records Commission, eight years on the Shelby County Historical Commission and four years on the Tennessee Historical Commission. During the 1980s, John produced and hosted a local history talk show on the public library's cable television channel.

In the private sector, Harkins served eight years as president of the West Tennessee Historical Society, two years as president of Descendants of Early Settlers of Shelby County and eight years in various offices on the board of the Davies Manor (museum home) Association. Over the decades, John has also held memberships in the Tennessee Historical Society, Memphis Heritage Inc., the Association for the Preservation of Tennessee Antiquities, the Tennessee Preservation Trust, the Jackson Purchase Historical Society and the Bartlett Historical Society.

Georgia S. Harkins has critiqued and edited virtually all of John's published works, and she remains his first and best critic. To her, he is most grateful.

Visit us at
www.historypress.net